It's All We Can Eat!

Scripture quotations marked TPT are from The Passion Translation. Copyright ©2017, 2018 by Passion & fire Ministries, Inc. Used by permission. All rights reserved.

Scripture quotations marked CEV are from the Contemporary English Version Copyright © 1991, 1992, 1995 by American Bible Society. Used by permission.

Scripture quotations marked HCSB are from the Holman Christian Standard Bible Copyright © 1999, 2000, 2002, 2003, 2009 by Holman Bible Publishers. Used by permission.

Scripture quotations marked Voice are from The Voice Copyright ©2008, by Ecclesia Bible Society. Used by permission. All rights reserved.

It's All We Can Eat!

Contents

Introduction: The Law Of Limitlessness

1 Fuel Up & Run Your Love Race!

2 It's All About Love!

3 Let's Talk About Love!

4 What's Love Got To Do With It?

5 Love Covers!

6 Love Liberates!

7 Love Makes Things Happen!

8 Love Demands Diligence!

9 Strengthened To Be Steadfast!

10 Guarded & Guided By Godliness

11 Born To Love & Assigned To Affection

12 Love Like The Lord!

13 Come And Get It!

14 Go Get It!

15 Revisiting The Very Reason

16 What Happens When We Love God's Way

It's "All We Can Eat!", Family. Let's Get It!

It's All We Can Eat!

It's All We Can Eat! Feasting On The Fruit Of The Spirit, Volume 2: Love by Robert L. Warring, Sr.

Published by Warring Global Publishing © Copyright 2020 All rights reserved.

ISBN: 978-0-9834514-1-9

This book or parts thereof may not be reproduced in any form, stored in a retrieval system, or transmitted in any form by any means - electronic, mechanical, photocopy, recording, or otherwise - without prior written permission of the publisher, except as provided by United States of America copyright law.

Unless otherwise noted, all Scripture quotations are taken from the Amplified Bible Classic Edition. Copyright © 1965, by The Lockman Foundation. Used by permission.

Scripture quotations marked AMP are from the Amplified Bible. Copyright © 1954, 1958, 1962, 1964, 1965, 1987 by The Lockman Foundation. Used by permission.

Scripture quotations marked by CJB are from The Complete Jewish Bible. Copyright © 1998 by David H. Stern. All rights reserved.

Scripture quotations ERV are from the Easy-to-Read Version of the Bible. Copyright © 2006 by World Bible Translation Center. Used by permission. All rights reserved.

Scripture quotations marked ESV are from the Holy Bible, English Standard Version. Copyright © 2001 by Crossway Bibles, a division of Good News Publishers. Used by permission. All rights reserved.

Scripture quotation marked EXB are from The Expanded Bible. Copyright © 2011 by Thomas Nelson, Inc. All rights reserved. Used by permission.

Scripture quotations marked GNT are from the Good News Translation (Today's English Version, Second Edition). Copyright © 1992 American Bible Society. All rights reserved.

Scripture quotations marked GW are taken from God's Word, Copyright © 1995 God's Word to the Nations. Used by permission of Baker Publishing Group.

Scripture quotations marked KJV are from the King James Version of the Bible.

Scripture quotations marked by MEV are from The Holy Bible, Modern English Version. Copyright © 2014 by Military Bible Association. Used by Permission.

Scripture quotations marked by MSG are from The Message: The Bible In Contemporary English, Copyright © 1983, 1994, 1995, 1996, 2000, 2001, 2002. Used by permission of NavPress Publishing Group.

Scripture quotations marked NKJV are taken from the New King James Version. Copyright 1982 but Thomas Nelson. Used by permission. All rights reserved.

Scripture quotations marked NLT are from the New Living Translation Copyright © 1996, 2004, 2007, 2013, 2015 by Tyndale House Foundation. Used by permission of Tyndale House Publishers, Inc. All rights reserved.

Scripture quotations marked NLV are from the New Life Version, Copyright © 1969 by Christian Literature International.

PART 1
Love Must Be Discovered & Demonstrate

Introduction
The Law Of Limitlessness

"But the fruit produced by the Holy Spirit within you is divine love in all its varied expressions: joy that overflows, peace that subdues, patience that endures, kindness in action, a life full of virtue, faith that prevails, gentleness of heart, and strength of spirit.
Never set the law above these qualities, for they are meant to be limitless."
(Galatians 5:22-23 TPT)

It's All We Can Eat!

Pile It On Your Plate!
"But the fruit produced by the Holy Spirit within you is…"

In the introduction of the first book of the series, *It's All We Can It! Volume 1: Fair & Legal*, I shared about a vision I had that inspired this book series. In my imagination I saw the image of someone walking away from a buffet table, at either a smorgasbord restaurant or on a cruise ship. My focus during this vision, was on an individual that walked away from the serving station, carefully measuring each step, with their plates *purposefully* piled high.

I shared that it's nothing wrong with it, since it was paid for. In fact, I was reminded of the many times that I have piled my plates high, with a plethora of whatever foods that pleased me – whether it was the familiar or unfamiliar fruit, desserts of other cultures, or cuisine from a different country, while on cruise ships.

I also shared how The Holy Spirit reminded me that we have the same sort of privilege, and that we should not be ashamed or embarrassed, because our meals are *already paid for*, and we can have *unlimited amounts* and *unobstructed access* to the buffet table of blessings! However, we must make sure that we're choosing the same menu items and have the same diet plan as The Lord, Who said, *"My food (nourishment) is to do the will (pleasure) of Him Who sent Me and to accomplish and completely finish His work."* (John 4:34)

What really blessed me as I was writing this chapter is that the Holy Spirit reminded me that we have reserved seating – *"And He raised us up together with Him and made us sit down together [giving us joint seating with Him] in the heavenly sphere [by virtue of our being] in Christ Jesus (the Messiah, the Anointed One)."* (Ephesians 2:6) Yup, we're in the VIP section: *Victorious, Inseparable, Predestined*!

He also reminded me that *"He offers a resting place for me in His luxurious love. His tracks take me to an oasis of peace, the quiet brook of bliss."* The Lord will also prepare a table for us in the presence of our enemies – He becomes *"my delicious feast even when my enemies dare to fight."* (see Psalm 23:2, 5 TPT)

What I taught in volume 1 is that one Greek word for fruit is *karpos*. Other meanings are *deed, action, a result,* and *gain*. According to the NAS Exhaustive Concordance, other translations for *"fruit"* are *crop* and *harvest*. Karpos can be used figuratively, as "everything done in true partnership with Christ." I also discovered that by this definition, *"fruit"* (karpos) results from two life streams – the Lord living His life through ours – to yield what is eternal."

Because karpos is specifically related to our *connection* to Christ, the following descriptions will be based on God's expectation of us – His Children or *fruit*. The word meanings above, are neutral. In other words, there are good deeds and there are bad deeds. There are good results, and bad results. You can have a good harvest, or you can have a bad harvest. There's good fruit, and is there's bad fruit.

In essence, The Holy Spirit *produces* the fruit, however it is our responsibility to *present* the fruit. In the same way that fruit starts out as a seed in the natural, the *fruit of the Spirit* starts out as a seed inside of us. It is *prepacked* in us once we accept Christ as our Lord and Savior. He prepares and produces on the *inside* of us what we present on the *outside* of us. However, it is our responsibility to *submit to* and *assist* in the cultivation of the seed, and to prepare ourselves for its production, by not preventing or precluding its growth and production.

We cannot do this by willpower, nor by physical strength. We need the *oil* or the anointing of The Lord.

"...Not by might, nor by power, but by My Spirit [of Whom the oil is a symbol], says the Lord of hosts." (Zechariah 4:6) We need God's help. It is a *predestined*, divine partnership. God embeds or implants the seed, and then we must embrace it, and exert effort in ensuring its growth. We can't contend with God, nor be counterproductive, or a contaminant.

This is why we are told, *"[Not in your own strength] for it is God Who is all the while effectually at work in you [energizing and creating in you the power and desire], both to will and to work for His good pleasure and satisfaction and delight."* (Philippians 2:13) The Passion Translation reads, *"Now you must continue to make this new life fully manifested...God will continually revitalize you, implanting within you the passion to do what pleases Him."* What pleases Him is when we produce or present an *abundant* harvest of fruit.

It is not enough just to produce or present fruit in any amount. Our Heavenly Father's preference and expectation is that we have a propensity for producing or presenting a *prolific* harvest! *"When you bear (produce) much fruit, My Father is honored and glorified, and you show and prove yourselves to be true followers of Mine." "When your lives bear abundant fruit, you demonstrate that you are My mature disciples who glorify My Father!"* (John 15:8 AMPC, TPT respectively, emphasis added) If we're satisfied with a "not much" mentality, we're not mature.

It is when we make it a *habit* of manifesting fruit in abundance, that we demonstrate our maturity. When we *proficiently produce fruit*, we praise and glorify God, and *prolifically prove* that we're disciples or devoted followers of, and branches *firmly fastened* to The True Vine. All the while, we're also prompting others to praise and glorify God. This is what it means to *"Let your light so shine before men that they may see your moral excellence and your praiseworthy, notable and good deeds and recognize and honor and praise and glorify your Father Who is in heaven."* (Matthew 5:16)

One thing that fascinates me about this fruit production process, is that the same fruit that we produce and present to God and others, is that very same *fruit* from which we feed off of or fuel ourselves with, for our assignments. Therefore, it is imperative that the fruit we produce and present, is a *healthy harvest* since it is from where we receive our health and nutrition!

Throughout the New Testament of the Bible, there are references to different types of athletics and occupations. There were fishermen, farmers, soldiers, wrestlers, and runners, etc. In order for them to be proficient at their specific station, they needed good health and nutrition. In other words, in order to be formidable and have a favorable outcome, nourishment – the *necessary fuel was needed*!

The same is true for us today. In order to be the force that our Father is calling us to be, and have favorable outcomes, it will require *fortitude* that can be found in the food or fruit we fuel up on. Therefore, we must load up or fuel up on foods that provide the highest *nutritional* value.

It's "All We Can Eat!", Family. Let's Live Limitless!

Chapter 1
Fuel Up & Run *Your* Race!

"Do you not know that in a race all runners run [their very best to win], but only one receives the prize? So run [your race] in such a way that you may seize the prize and make it yours!"
(1 Corinthians 9:24)

Although it is not my intention to cause confusion or controversy, some statements that I write or comments that I make, may conflict with your interpretation or translation of the Bible. However, my hope is that at the culmination of each chapter, you will conclude that what was written, was encouraging, inspiring and informative.

I felt that it was necessary to make this disclaimer because chapter one includes some ideas and concepts that may clash with your theology, or what you understand or interpret the Bible verse to mean. I promise you that I am not a heretic, I do not spread heresy, and that I did, in fact, hear from The Holy Spirit, while writing this volume.

According to the Dake Annotated Reference Bible, the fruit of the Spirit can be referred to as "Manifestations of a spiritual life." I also found it interesting that in my English Standard Version (ESV) Bible, the Scripture text that forms the basis of this book, falls in the category of or under the chapter heading, "Keep In Step With The Spirit." The New King James Version has their heading of that section of the chapter of Galatians 5:22-24 as "Walking in the Spirit."

Although it is a good and admirable goal to walk with the Spirit, our ultimate goal should be to *keep in step* with the Spirit. In order to achieve optimum performance and accomplish what God has planned for us, we must *keep pace* with The Spirit, as well as *be fueled by* the fruit of the Spirit. It is imperative that we do this because there are those who are watching us, as well as those who are waiting on us, in order for them to discover their purpose and reach their destiny.

"Therefore then, since we are surrounded by so great a cloud of witnesses [who have borne testimony to the Truth...let us run with patient endurance and steady and active persistence the appointed course of the race that is set before us," (see Hebrews 12:1)

The Passion Translation renders the last part of that verse, *"Then we will be able to run life's marathon race with passion and determination, for the path has been already marked out before us."* The footnote for that verse indicates that "the Aramaic can be translated, *'the race [personally] appointed to us.'* God has the destiny for each of us that we are to give ourselves fully to reach." Not only has the path *already* been marked out for us, but the *pace* has already been set for us, as well!

Our preoccupation should be to *"run with passion into His abundance so that I may reach the purpose that Jesus Christ has called me to fulfill and wants me to discover."* "I press on toward the goal to win the [supreme and heavenly] prize to which God in Christ Jesus is calling the upward." (see Philippians 3:12 TPT; 3:14 AMPC respectively emphasis added) This pressing and pursuing purpose and the prize, should include answering the call to produce an abundance of fruit.

Whether we see ourselves as farmers, fishermen, soldiers, wrestlers, or runners; our assignment requires that we consume food for fuel or energy in our endeavors. I recommend that we fuel up on the Love or *the fruit of the Spirit*. As long as we remain connected Christ – *"The True Vine"*, we'll have an *inexhaustible supply*, to fortify us for our assignments!

It's "All We Can Eat!", Family. Let's Fuel Up & Run Our Race!

Chapter 2
It's All About Love

"But the fruit produced by the Holy Spirit within you is divine love in all its varied expressions: joy that overflows, peace that subdues, patience that endures, kindness in action, a life full of virtue, faith that prevails, gentleness of heart, and strength of spirit.
Never set the law above these qualities, for they are meant to be limitless."
(Galatians 5:22-23 TPT)

It's All We Can Eat!

As I mentioned in the introduction, a Greek word for *"fruit"* is *karpos*. Other meanings are "action, crop, deed, a result, harvest, profit", and "gain." So, in essence, the Scripture could have been translated, "The action of the Holy Spirit is…", "The deeds of the Holy Spirit are…", "A result of the Spirit is...", or "The harvest of the Spirit is…", etc.

Something was spoken – a seed was sown – a principle was preached that prompted me to write this chapter. It is the result of reading about when The Lord Jesus said, *"I am the True Vine, and My Father is the Vinedresser. Dwell in Me, and I will dwell in you. [Live in Me, and I will live in you.] Just as no branch can bear fruit of itself without abiding in (being vitally united to) the vine, neither can you bear fruit unless you abide in Me. I am the Vine; you are the branches. Whoever lives in Me and I in him bears much (abundant) fruit. However, apart from Me [cut off from vital union with Me] you can do nothing."* (John 15:1, 4-5)

The Greek word for *"Vinedresser"* is *georgos* (gheh-ore-gos). It's defined as "husbandman" and also means "a worker of the soil, gardener" and "farmer." He's the one in charge, *whose primary function is to get the most fruit production* – the *maximum yield* from the branches. In the very beginning of mankind, we were scooped up from the *soil*. It is written, *"Then the Lord God formed [that is, created the body of] man from the dust of the ground, and breathed into his nostrils the breath [or Spirit] of life; and the man became a living being [an individual complete in body and spirit]."* (Genesis 2:7 AMP)

As the Husbandman, our Heavenly Father expects us to be *profitable* and *produce a gain,* by yielding or having a *healthy* and *huge* harvest. The first step in making sure that we do, is by remaining *"vitally united to"* the *"True Vine."* He is where we get our *nourishment*. The next step in making sure that we have a *huge* harvest is by remaining *"vitally united to"* the *"True Vine." He* is where we get our provision to produce and *flourish*. Did you catch that? It wasn't a typo. At the risk of appearing to be redundant, I repeated it. We must view our *"vital union"* or connection to Christ, as *critical* or *crucial* as an umbilical cord is to an embryo!

Caution: Sharp Curve!

And now, we come to the first controversial corner. The Message interpretation begins Galatians 5:22 by asking, *"But what happens when we live God's way?"* I first, want to address what *"God's way"* is. Living God's way is living by the Spirit of God or being led by the Holy Spirit. *"For in Him we live and move and have our being;"* (see Acts 17:28) *"It is through him that we live and function and have our identity;"* (TPT) Let's just say it's living "righteously" or "in right standing with God." We live *in* and *through* Him, and He lives *in* and *through* us!

The Greek word for *"move"* is *kineo* (kin-eh-o). It can mean "provoke, stir" and "way". It's from where the English word *kinetic* is derived, which means "of or relating to the motion of material bodies and the forces and energy associated therewith." It can also mean *active, dynamic, energizing,* lively motion, or movement. So as you can see, it was never God's intention for us to just sit still, become stagnant, or remain sedentary.

The Greek word for *"being"* is *eimi* (i-mee). It can mean (I) "am, (we) are, appear, belong, gain, exist, give thyself wholly to, have been, have hope, live long," and "will be." So, I guess you could say, "It is in Him that we live, are stirred, make our way, appear, belong, exist, have hope" and "will be!" Yes, in Him, give ourselves wholly to. Praise Break: HALLELUJAH!!!

In using The Passion Translation, I intentionally drew a distinction between this version and others. Most

Bible translations begin Galatians 5:22, *"But the fruit of the Spirit is love..."* However, The Passion Translation is decidedly different. The key phrase in the verse is, *"...divine love in all its varied expressions:..."* The footnotes offer this explanation: "There is clear textual inference that the 'fruit' (singular) of the Holy Spirit is love, with other virtues displaying aspects of the greatest quality of Spirit-life, *agape* love."

Two things are clear to me. One, is that there *aren't* nine different fruits of the Spirit. <u>There's only one *"fruit"* or *"harvest"* that is produced</u>. The second thing, is that this *"fruit"* or *"harvest"* is found in, or flows from the Spirit of God – the Holy Spirit, and as we all know; *"God is love."* (see 1 John 4:7-8) Therefore, we could say, "But the fruit or harvest produced by the Holy Spirit within us is His love, which is expressed in various versions or forms of *love*, such as *joy, peace, patience...*" As I stated in the introduction, according to the Dake Annotated Reference Bible, the fruit of the Spirit can be referred to as "Manifestations of a spiritual life."

The Spirit of God is more than just a Fruit Producer or Heaven's Harvest Maker. Although He is known as *"the Lord of the Harvest"* and *"Owner of the Harvest"* (see Matthew 9:38), we are taught, *"for it is He Himself Who gives life and breath and all things to all [people]..."* (Acts 17:25) With this life that we're given or gifted, we get to *live* it, *operating* or *flowing* in the various versions of His love; as both, *givers and receivers* of it!

Blessed, And Highly Flavored!

While preparing to teach Bible Study one night, the Holy Spirit gave me a revelation concerning the fruit of the Spirit, or the *various expressions of His love*. Do you remember the book *Charlie & The Chocolate Factory* or the movie *Willy Wonka & The Chocolate Factory*? In the story, there was a candy created or invented by Willy Wonka, the founder of the chocolate factory.

There were all kinds of candy in the chocolate factory, but there was one special concoction of candy called the "Everlasting Gobstopper." This candy not only changed colors, but it also *changed flavors*, when it was consumed! What was also fascinating about this confection, was that it *never got any smaller or disappeared*! When I was a child, I *wished* that I had that candy!

The fruit of the Spirit is sort of like the Everlasting Gobstopper, except that the fruit of the Spirit is *real*! It is one main fruit, with multiple flavors. In other words, its eight *expressions* or *flavors* of the Spirit of Love, flowing from one *Source*. For example, in The Holy Trinity there's The Father, The Son, and The Holy Spirit; yet *They Are All One*!

Similarly, The Lord can reveal Himself to us as *Jehovah Rophe* (our Healer), *Jehovah Tsidkenu* (our Righteousness), or *Jehovah Shalom* (our Peace). He is *still* God, no matter how He reveals Himself or shows up in our lives, which varies, depending on our circumstances and situations. In the same way, *the fruit of the Spirit* is Love, with eight different *flavors*, *colors* or *manifestations* of Love.

It's "All We Can Eat!", Family. Let's Enjoy All Of The Expressions!

Chapter 3
Let's Talk About Love!

"The Spirit, on the other hand, brings a harvest of love, joy, peace; patience towards others, kindness, benevolence; good faith, meekness, self-restraint. Against such things as these there is no law..."
(Galatians 5:22-24 WNT)

In a later chapter, I characterize love as a *covering* or *coating*, and since I'm referring to fruit; perhaps, I should have added *peeling*. I concluded this, after reading Colossians 3:14, which reads, *"And above all these [put on] love and enfold yourselves with the bond of perfectness [which binds everything together completely in ideal harmony]."* (emphasis added)

Before I could effectively write and teach about love, as referenced in Galatians 5:22, I had to go back to research and learn more about love, as referenced in Colossians 3:14. Otherwise, I would have done you and myself a huge disservice. I don't like missing out on opportunities to learn and teach. Now that I've learned something else, I can elaborate on it.

By beginning with *"And above all these [put on] love and enfold yourselves…"*, the Apostle Paul was pointing out to them (the church at Colosse) and us, that they were (and we are) to *"put on"* as a *priority*, this type of love. I believe The Passion Translation speaks to why it *must be a priority*. It reads, *"For love is supreme and must flow through each of these virtues. Love becomes the mark of true maturity"* (emphasis added)

This expression of love is *agape* (ag-ah-pay). It means "benevolence, charity, esteem," and "goodwill." It is the type of love which centers in moral preference. It is divine love – the God *quality*, or the love that God *prefers*. It's the *unconditional* love of God. Similar to altruism, it is devoted to, or *seeks the highest good* of others. It's not *feelings-focused*, nor based on attitude or emotion. This *expression* of love includes a *commitment to the welfare* or well-being of others without any conditions or circumstances. As stated, it means "goodwill." However, I'd like to think of it as *God's Will*! It's the love from which *all other* forms of love are birthed or *flow*.

Even more than the *God Quality* or love that God prefers, it is the *"greatest."* The Apostle Paul wrote, *"And now there remain: faith [abiding trust in God and His promises], hope [confident expectation of eternal salvation], love [<u>unselfish love for others growing out of God's love for me</u>], these three [the choices graces]; <u>but the greatest of these is love</u>."* (1 Corinthians 13:13 AMP emphasis added) This is because faith and hope *flow from love*. Also, faith and hope have an expiration date – they're temporary. However, love is *eternal*! The Passion Translation reads, *"…Yet love surpasses them all. So above all else, let love be the beautiful prize for which you run."* The latter part of that verse is actually the beginning of verse one of chapter fourteen in most Bible translations. Nevertheless, this is the love that *we should all aim at attaining*.

Similar to the eight expressions of love or fruit of the Spirit in Galatians 5:22-23, here in 1 Corinthians chapter 13, the Apostle Paul lists or points out ten characteristics or descriptions of divine love. They are patience under pressure, consistent kindness, generosity/gentleness (never jealous), humility, courteousness, unselfishness (not manipulative or controlling), cordial or friendly (not easily offended), sincere (scrupulous), rejoices in righteousness, and loyal.

We are not only to put on this type of love, but in Colossians 3:14, he instructed us to *"enfold"* ourselves in it. To *"enfold"* means to "bundle, envelope, surround, tighten" or "wrap" yourself with a *covering*, such as a blanket, cloak, coat, etc. Not only are we to *"enfold"* ourselves in this love, but we must also do so, *for the duration of the process*, or God's designated time of *"perfectness."*

It's All We Can Eat!

The Greek word for *"perfectness"* is *teleiotes* (tel-i-ot-ace). It can mean "completeness, perfection, maturity" and "to the end." It's related to the Greek word *telesphoreo* (tel-es-for-eh-o), which means "to be a bearer to completion (maturity), to ripen fruit – bring fruit to perfection." If I had a microphone, I would have dropped it right here!

There's another part to this process that is necessary in order to arrive at or reach maturity – *produce ripe fruit*. However, to explain it, I had to view it from another version of Colossians 3:14: *"Beyond all these things put on and wrap yourselves in [unselfish] love, which is the perfect bond of unity [for everything is bound together in agreement when each one seeks the best for others]."* (AMP emphasis added).

Show Him What You're Working With!

In my Study Bible notes, a commentator stated, "As we clothe ourselves with these virtues, the last garment we are to put on is love, which holds all of the others in place. To practice any list of virtues without practicing love will lead to distortion, fragmentation, and stagnation." They reference 1 Corinthians 13:3, which reads, *"And if I were to be so generous as to give away everything I owned to feed the poor, and to offer my body to be burned as a martyr, without the pure motive of love, I would gain nothing of value."* (TPT emphasis added) The AMPC reads, *"...but have not love (God's love in me), I gain nothing."*

In some texts, the Aramaic word used for *"burn"* is a homonym that can mean either to burn or to "boast." Because of this, some Bible translations use the phrase "I offer my body in order to boast [glory]." I believe he wrote this, because he realized and wanted to relay to them (and to us) that love *"is not boastful or vainglorious, does not display itself haughtily"* (see 1 Corinthians 13:4). Anything we do that is not motivated by love and to glorify God, will

It's All We Can Eat!

be viewed by Him as *valueless*. When we use our gifts or platforms to point to or glorify ourselves, or as a stage to perform for others to see us, God sees it as *useless* and *pointless*!

When the Apostle Paul wrote to the church at Corinth (and us), he explained that even if he could expound on matters with eloquence, speak with the language of angels, articulate the amazing mysteries of God (The Warring Paraphrase), *"but have not love (that reasoning, <u>intentional, spiritual devotion such as is inspired by God's love for and in us</u>), I am only a noisy gong or a clanging cymbal...I am nothing (a useless nobody)."* (see 1 Corinthians 13:1-2 emphasis added)

The Amplified version of the end of verse one reads, *"...then I have become only a noisy gong or a clanging cymbal [just an annoying distraction]."* What's interesting about the cymbal that he references is that *two* of them must be struck together to make *music*. Otherwise, it's just a loud noise. In the same way, our gifts and actions must work in concert with or be *motivated by love,* in order to *make music* that is pleasing to God's ears. Otherwise, without love, it's nothing more than meaningless *noise*!

Again, this is *agape love* – the *God quality*, the *highest* form of love. The Aramaic word for love is *hooba*. According to The Passion Translation commentary, it means "to set on fire." The concept is that it is a "burning" or "fiery love" that originates "in the inner depths of the heart as an eternal energy, an active power of bonding hearts and lives in secure relationships." I suppose this is the sentiment that the sons of Korah had, when they sang, *"My heart is on fire, boiling over with passion. Bubbling up within me are these beautiful lyrics as a lovely poem to be sung for the King. Like a river bursting its banks, I'm overflowing with words, spilling out into this sacred story."* (Psalm 45:1 TPT)

It's All We Can Eat!

This *should not* be an unusual occurrence for us. We should *always express* this level of love – not only for God, but for others, as well. We are instructed, *"Above all, <u>have fervent and unfailing love for one another, because love covers</u> a multitude of sins [it overlooks unkindness and <u>unselfishly seeks the best for others</u>]."* (1 Peter 4:8) *"Above all, <u>constantly echo God's intense love</u> for one another..."* (AMP and TPT respectively, emphasis added) This reminds me of when I first got saved and would hear people say that they were "on fire for Jesus!" I'll elaborate on this verse in another chapter.

It's "All We Can Eat!", Family. Let's Show Him What We're Working With!

It's All We Can Eat!

Chapter 4
What's *Love* Got To Do With It?!

*"Most of all, love each other as if your life depended on it.
Love makes up for practically anything."*
(1 Peter 4:8 MSG)

In the last chapter, I left off with the statement about how I used to hear others say that they were "on fire for Jesus." If I may be transparent for a moment, it wasn't until a recent radio interview, that I publicly revealed that I had not been living with such *passion* – that I felt like I was *on fire for the Lord*, until a year or so ago (2020), when I started studying, and writing about the fruit of the Spirit. I recall revealing to the radio host, "I'm in love again!"

Somewhere in my 30 years of being a Christian, I had lost my passion. However, lately (the past 2 years), I have learned that I am called to lead by example, and also to *lead with love*. In short, I am to be an *"imitator"* of Christ. He led by example and He also led with love because He *is* Love! Here are some ways that Christ exemplified this *expression* of His love: *"I have loved you just as the Father has loved Me; remain in My love [and do not doubt My love for you]."* (John 15:9 AMP emphasis added)

The Passion Translation reads, *"I love each of you with the same love that the Father loves me. You must continually let my love nourish your hearts. If you keep my commands, you will live in my love, just as I have kept my Father's commands, for I continually live nourished and empowered by His love. My purpose for telling you these things is so that the joy that I experience will fill your hearts with overflowing gladness!"* (John 15:9-11 TPT emphasis added) It was this passage of Scripture that *shook me at my core*, during the pandemic, and ushered be back into the love that I had lost! When I read it, *seemingly* for the first time, I realized that I wasn't loving *this* way – His way!

The requirement is that we love one another with the *"same love"* quality or brand that our Father has for The Son and The Son has for His Father; especially since this is the *"same love"* brand or quality with which the Lord Jesus loves us. The only way to obtain and maintain this level of love is by the power of the Holy Spirit, Who helps us remain connected and *"continually nourished"* by Christ.

He explained that *this was how* He was able to *"continually live nourished and empowered."* In addition to experiencing a continual flow of nourishment and power, the Lord explained that He wanted the disciples' (and our) hearts to experience, be filled with, and enveloped in the same power, nourishment, and *"overflowing gladness"*; which is another *expression of love* that I will cover in another volume.

God is not asking us to *share* our love that He gave us with others. He is *commanding* us to *serve* His love to others. Initially, I was going to write that He wants us to share it. However, that would require that we render or relinquish what was *ours*. That's not the case.

In a sense, it's sort of like when a parent gives money to the older child, for them to go to the store with their younger sibling, and tells the child to give the younger sibling *their portion* of the money. The money belongs to the parent, but they gave it to *both*, although the more *mature one* is responsible for disbursing the money. They are not sharing the money with their sibling, because it was *never their money* to begin with. They are s*erving* their sibling *their share* of the money.

Another scenario would be the parent preparing the meal, and then telling the *mature* child to fix their plate and also fix another plate and serve it to their sibling. Again, they are not sharing their meal with their sibling, because it was *never their meal* to begin with. They are merely s*erving* the meal to their sibling. The Lord said, *"...My food (nourishment) is to do the will (pleasure) of Him Who sent Me and to accomplish and completely finish His work."* (John 4:34) This *"food"* or meal is also on our menu, and we are expected to *"accomplish and completely finish His* *work"*, by loving others with the *same love* that The Lord loves us, and The Father loves Him.

This *"same love"* quality of love is what I call *one love* or *oneness* love. This is the love that the Lord prayed we would *live in*, when He prayed to our Heavenly Father, *"That they all may be one, [just] as You, Father, are in Me and I in You, that <u>they also may be one in Us</u>, so that the world may believe and be convinced that You have sent Me."* (John 17:21 emphasis added) The Passion Translation reads, *"I pray for them all to <u>be joined together as one</u> even as you and I, Father, are joined together as one."* (emphasis added)

Supreme Love

It astonishes me that The Architect of the Universe would ask the Almighty God to *include* us in the same quality of Supreme Love that He shared with the Father. There's not a greater quality love than this. He not only laid down His Life for us, but He also asked our Father to share Their Supreme Love with *us*!

We are called to be imitators of God. Therefore, here are a few ways we can exemplify God's love: *"...Love each other deeply, as much as I have loved you. For the greatest love of all is a love that sacrifices all. And this great love is demonstrated when a person sacrifices his life for his friends."* (John 15:12-13 TPT) If we're not loving others and ourselves deeply and sacrificially, we're not loving the way God loves.

"Therefore be imitators of God [copy Him and follow His example, as well-beloved children [imitate their father]. And walk in love, [esteeming and delighting in one another] as Christ loved us and gave Himself up for us, a slain offering and sacrifice to God [for you, so that it became] a sweet fragrance." (Ephesians 5:1-2) Verse two in The Passion

Translation reads, *"And continue to walk surrendered to the extravagant love of Christ…"*

"Beloved, let us [unselfishly] love and seek the best for one another, for love is from God; and everyone who loves [others] is born of God and knows God [through personal experience]. By this the love of God was displayed in us…so that we might live through Him. Beloved, if God so loved us [in this incredible way], we also ought to love one another." (see 1 John 4:7-12 AMP) We can't live through Him, unless we *love* through Him, and let His love live in and *through* us!

In other words, Divinely loved ones, let us love each other with the quality of love that God loves us with. This love is birthed in and flows from God. They that love like this – that love like their Father, prove that they were born of and live for Him. If He loved us so extravagantly, passionately, and sacrificially; we should also love each other so extravagantly, passionately, and sacrificially.

When we love this way, we identify with Him and prove that we are born of or have our origin in Him, have sonship from Him, we know Him, we are intimate with Him, we love Him, we have our identity in Him, and we are obedient to Him. It also proves that we are paying the debt or obligation that we owe. The Greek word for *"ought"* in 1 John 4:11 is *opheilo* (of-i-lo). It means "to owe, be indebted, obliged to rectify a debt." It's a reference to "being morally obligated (or legally required) to meet an obligation, i.e., to pay off a legitimate debt."

Every child has their father's DNA. Therefore, they have some of their father's features. They may either look like their father, walk like their father, talk / sound like their father, etc. One of the greatest compliments that a father can hear is when someone sees their child and says to the father's child, "You look *just like* your daddy!" or "You have your father's eyes!" In the same sense, our Heavenly Father feels complimented when someone sees His features in us. It glorifies God when we *resemble* and *represent* Him in how we *"love one another."* It blesses His heart when others say. "You love *just like* your Daddy!"

Love Makes Things Happen!

Unfortunately, some people seem to believe that love is just an emotion or feeling and that's all. They also seem to think that love doesn't have to be demonstrated or expressed unless they *feel like it.* However, nothing could be farther from the truth or *The Truth*! Love is a decision or choice, accompanied by actions that are activated or motivated by the love of God – the fruit of the Spirit. The Lord Jesus said, *"Loving me empowers you to obey my commands."* (TPT) Obedience in an activity. Obedience is *love in action*! The Amplified Classic Edition reads, *"If you [really] love Me, you will keep (obey) My commands."* (John 14:15) So, as we can see from The Lord Himself, He has empowered us to *act* and *do*, not just to *feel*! Love demands *demonstration*!

Although *agape* love originates on, and emanates from the inside – even though it is an intense internal affection, it must be demonstrated externally and *eternally*. As we saw in Psalm 45, the description was *"boiling over with passion."* There was also *"Bubbling up"*, *"Like a river bursting its banks,"*, *"overflowing"*, and *"spilling out into..."* These sons of Korah were describing their experience with expressing their lyrics of a song or poem about the Lord – their King. However, we are not only to use *words* and *lyrics* to express our love of God and love for one another; we are expected to express our love *with our lives*! With our lives and actions, the love of God should boil over, bubble up, burst out, overflow, and spill into the lives of others – *over and over*! This is what I refer to as a *fervent and effectual* love life or lifestyle.

It's All We Can Eat!

Being fervent and effectual is not just limited to how we love and live life. The expectation is that we also pray this way. We are told, *"The earnest (heartfelt, continued) prayer of a righteous man makes tremendous power available [dynamic in its working]."* (James 5:16b) *"The effectual fervent prayer of a righteous man availeth much."* (KJV) The Passion Translation reads, *"...for <u>tremendous power is released through the passionate, heartfelt prayer of a godly believer!</u>"* (emphasis added) The Greek word for *"effectual"* is *energeo* (en-erg-eh-o). It means "to be active, efficient" and "be mighty in." It is closely related to the word *energeia* (en-erg-i-ah), which means "efficiency" and from where we get our word *energy*. It is also closely related to the word *energes* (en-er-gace), which means "operative, powerful."

The reason I'm taking my time right here, is because the Holy Spirit was teaching me something, as I was studying and writing the previous few paragraphs. The Greek word for *"fervent"* is *zeo* (dzeh-o). It means "to be hot, boil (of liquids), glow (of solids)" and "to be earnest." It is also used metaphorically as "boiling with love, zeal, for what is good", as well as "to bubble over."

In Acts 12:5, it is written about those disciples who were interceding for Peter that *"fervent prayer for him was persistently made."* The Greek word used here, is *ektenos* (ek-ten-oce). It means "intent" which is derived from the word *ektenes* (ek-ten-ace), meaning "intently" and "without ceasing." Another word that is related, is *ekteleo* (ek-tel-eh-o). It means "to complete –fully finish." These words can be traced back to the root word *ekteino* (ek-ti-no), which means "to stretch, extend, put forth" and "stretch out."

Based on my research and what I remember about God's *brand* or quality of love, I believe that like our prayer life, our love life should *boil over*, *bubble up*, and *glow*. Love *demands* displays and demonstrations! Therefore, we should be willing to stretch out – extend ourselves to others, with love; bringing it to *completion* or until it is *fully finished*. I'm reminded of The Lord's command for us to *go the extra mile*. He said, *"And if anyone forces you to go one mile, go with him two [miles]."* (Matthew 5:41) If we are commanded to have this attitude towards those who take advantage of us and mistreat us, how much more should we have this attitude and affection towards our brothers and sisters who are Believers, who aren't adversarial?

I have this idea in my head that is inescapable. The idea is that the love that we're instructed to demonstrate is inextricably tied to or intrinsic to the attributes of the Word of God (Love). Our love should flow the same way that agape love flows and functions. Agape love is effectual, fervent, active, energizing, overflows, and should spill into the lives of others; *"...the word that God speaks is alive <u>and full of power</u> [making it <u>active, operative, energizing, and effective</u>...penetrating to the dividing line of the breath of life (soul) and [the immortal] spirit... <u>[of the deepest parts of our nature]</u> ..."* (see Hebrews 4:12 emphasis added)

It is demonstrated *externally* by the deeds or works that we do, because of the Love working *internally*! We are told, *"...our love can't be an abstract theory we only talk about, <u>but a way of life demonstrated through our loving deeds</u>."* (1 John 3:18 TPT emphasis added) I believe that in the same way that faith without works is dead, *love without works or actions is dead*! The only thing that should be dead in us is our *old man* and *law* (Romans 6).

This power or virtue called love can only be validated and add value to others by our outward actions. *"So also faith, if it does not have works (deeds and actions of obedience to back it up), by itself is destitute of power [inoperative, dead]."* (James 2:17) The Message reads,

It's All We Can Eat!

"Isn't it obvious that God-talk without God-acts is outrageous nonsense?" The Passion Translation reads, *"So then faith that doesn't involve action is phony."* (emphasis added)

Those Scriptures remind me of the song by James Brown, "Talkin' Loud and Sayin' Nothing". My actions and my love must be *louder* than my words! I realize that the only way I can live and love the way God commanded, is to live with the same purpose that the Apostle Paul suggested when he wrote, *"...and the life I now live in the body I live by faith in (adherence to and reliance on and complete trust in) the Son of God, Who loved me and gave Himself up for me."* (Galatians 2:20)

Not only must our love be *demonstrated* – it must also be *proven*. *"If you consider yourself to be wise and one who understands the ways of God, advertise it with a beautiful, fruitful life guided by wisdom's gentleness. Never brag or boast about what you've done and you'll prove that you're truly wise."* (James 3:13 TPT) We don't advertise with our enticing words, but by our excellent deeds. The Apostle Paul wrote, *"And my speech and my preaching was not with enticing words of man's wisdom, but in the demonstration of the Spirit and of power:"* (1 Corinthians 2:4 KJV) In other words, we don't prove our worth, influence, or wisdom with enticing words – we don't prove or demonstrate how dope or deep we are, with slick words, but *by the fruit of the Spirit!*

We prove our love by *what* and *how* we perform, and that is with *love, gentleness*, and *humility*. The word Greek word used for *"beautiful"* is *kalos* (kal-os). It means "an outward sign of that inward good, noble, honorable character." It inspires or motivates others to embrace what is lovely. As someone once said, "Preach the Gospel, and if necessary, use words."

Some meanings for prove are "to show, convince, make credible, represent as good" and "put to the test." We are commanded, *"Conduct yourselves properly (honorably, righteously) ...so that...they may by <u>witnessing your good deeds</u> [come to] glorify God..." "Live <u>honorable lives</u> as you mix with unbelievers...For they will <u>see your beautiful works</u> and have a reason to glorify God"* (see 1 Peter 2:12 AMPC, TPT emphasis added). It's letting or allowing our *"light so shine"* that we are instructed to do, in Matthew 5:16. People witness, inspect or examine, and are inspired or motivated by what is *seen and experienced* – not what is said or explained to them. Then, they have a *"reason to"* reverence or glorify God! Our love will be tested and evaluated. Prayerfully, it results in a powerful testimony of the goodness of God.

It's *"All We Can Eat!"*, Family. Let's Love Supremely!

Chapter 5
Love Covers!

"Most of all, love each other steadily and unselfishly, because love makes up for many faults."
(1 Peter 4:8 VOICE)

Although I didn't have full comprehension of the concept when I characterized this love as a covering, coating, or perhaps, even a *peeling* (fruit); I now have a clearer understanding of *why*! That's because I discovered that the Greek word used for *"bond"* is *sundesmos* (soon-des-mos). It is defined as "that which binds together." It can also mean "joint tie, ligament, uniting principle" and "control." *Sundesmos* is closely related to the Greek word *syndesmos*, which can mean "a close (inner) identity which produces close harmony between members joined closely together."

These definitions remind me and also give me a better understanding of what the Apostle Paul meant when he wrote to the Ephesians church, *"For because of Him the whole body (the church, in all its various parts), closely joined and firmly knit together by the joints and ligaments with which it is supplied, when each part [with power adapted to its need] is working properly [in all its functions], grows to full maturity, building itself up in love."* (Ephesians 4:16)

When we are living in, operating in, producing, or presenting the fruit of the Spirit (love); we summon or permit another spirit to appear. When we're living life inspired by the fruit of the Spirit, we invite or invoke the *"spirit of unity."* When the Apostle Paul penned the letter to the church in Rome, he wrote to them (and to us), *"May the God who gives endurance and encouragement give you <u>a spirit of unity</u> among yourselves as you follow Christ Jesus,"* (Romans 15:5 NIV emphasis added)

According to the commentary of Colossians 3:14 in the Dake Annotated Reference Bible, "Divine love is to be put on as the outer garment and finishing touch to a well-dressed Christian. After putting on the eight other things of note, one is to put on this outer cloak as the bond of perfectness or as a girdle. It is to cover all, unite all, and bind all together as one. This is true perfection."

When it comes to the spirit of unity, there is nothing we can't do together. It is written, *"And the Lord said, 'Behold, they are one people, and they have all one language; and this is only the beginning of what they will do, and now nothing they have imagined they can do will be impossible for them."* (Genesis 11:7) When we operate in unity, we experience power and success. We also experience the blessing of God because He commands it when and where we come together. *"Behold, how good and how pleasant it is for brethren to dwell together in unity! ...for there the Lord has commanded the blessing, even life for evermore [upon the high and the lowly]."* (see Psalm 133)

Love Is A Covering
*"Above all, constantly echo God's intense love for one another,
for love will be a canopy over a multitude of sins."*
(1 Peter 4:8 TPT)

As I continue with this concept of love being a *covering*, I feel compelled to insert a command of God, concerning how we ought – how we're *called* to live. The command begins with, *"[Live] as children of obedience [to God];...as the One Who called you is holy, you yourselves also be holy in all your conduct and manner of living. For it is written, You shall be holy, for I am holy."* (1 Peter 1:14-16) I believe that since we are commanded to be holy, for God (Love) is holy; in the same respect, we are called to be a *covering*, for God is a covering – we are to *cover*, because God (Love) covers! I also believe that love is a covering. Therefore, Love (God) *loves* (covers)!

Now, let's dive deeper into the depths, definitions, and descriptions of *cover* and *covering*. In doing so, I'll expound on 1 Peter 4:8. The Greek word *"echo"* (used above), means to "have, hold, keep" or "possess." When digging deeper into the etymology of echo, I discovered that as a verb, it means "to call to mind." As a noun, it means "a close parallel of the feeling, idea, style", "a reply that repeats what has just been said", and "a repetition or imitation of another."

This reminds me of two commands given to us. The first is, *"...be imitators of God [copy Him and follow His example], as well-beloved children [imitate their father]. And walk in love, [esteeming and delighting in one another] as Christ loved us and gave Himself up for us..."* (Ephesians 5:1-2) The second one is, *"Let this same attitude and purpose and [humble] mind be in you which was also in Christ: [let Him be your example in humility:]"* (Philippians 2:5) The Passion Translation reads, *"...Let His mindset become your motivation."*

We get another glimpse of our Master's mindset by looking at John 5:19, which reads, *"...The Son is not able to do anything from himself or through my own initiative. I only do the works that I see the Father doing, for the Son does the same works as his Father."* (TPT) In other words, we must reiterate the *rich, intense* love from our Father – not only by repeating or echoing it back to Him, but also by echoing it – *acting it out* to one another, as well! In the same way that our Savior emulated The Almighty, we must echo, imitate, or emulate Emmanuel.

You may know someone skeptical who might say, "But I don't see Him, or *the works* He's doing." If that is the case, tell them the same thing that Paul told Timothy. He wrote, *"Imitate me, as I also imitate Christ."* (1 Corinthians 11:1 NKJV) I promise you that I'm not trying to put any pressure on you. However, the implication is that they should see *us* doing some of *"the works"* He's doing, in order for them to not only *imitate* us, but also see, glorify, and eventually emulate Him, as well!

We're supposed to freely give away what was feely given to us. In return for what we have received, we are to replicate or redistribute it. In my imagination, I see love as a medicine or a *controlled substance*, and I see myself as someone who should being charged with *possession with the intent to distribute*. I'm guilty, as charged!

As 1 Peter 4:8 encourages us to *"constantly echo"* God's love, it describes the degree or grade of love as being *"intense."* Many translations read, *"fervent."* As I wrote earlier, the Greek word used, is *ekteino* (ek-ti-no), which means "to stretch, extend, put forth" and "stretch out." Figuratively, it means "zealous, earnest." It can also mean "fully extended, at maximum potential" and "without slack." From the Old French intense, it means "extreme" and "great." From the Latin intensus, we get "stretched, strained" and "tight." I believe that if God were to command us with colloquialisms, He would say, "Keep your love *tight* for one another." or "Have *extreme* love for each other."

As I researched the words related to this concept of covering – especially *stretched*, *tight*, and *fully extended*; I kept getting an image in my mind of an awning or canopy. I was then reminded of the times that I would run under one to seek refuge from the rain, or resort to resting or taking shelter in the shade under one, when the sun was shining bright and the outside temperature was hot. Just as an awning or canopy can provide comfort, shelter, or covering; Love does the same thing, except that Love *lasts longer*! *"Those*

It's All We Can Eat!

who live in the shelter of the Most High will find rest in the shadow of the Almighty. This I declare about the LORD: he alone is my refuge, my place of safety; he is my God, and I trust him." (Psalm 91:1-2 NLT)

If you're wondering how long Love *extends*, *lasts*, or *stretches*; take a look at what I read one morning, during my devotional reading: *"But Lord, your endless love stretches from one eternity to the other, unbroken and unrelenting towards those who fear you and those who bow face down in awe before you. Your faithfulness to keep every gracious promise you've made passes from parents, to children, to grandchildren, and beyond."* (Psalm 103:17 TPT emphasis added)

1 Peter 4:8 concludes, *"for love will be a canopy over a multitude of sins."* (TPT) Other versions read, *"...for love covers a multitude of sins [forgives and disregards the offenses of others]."* (AMPC) *"...it overlooks unkindness and unselfishly seeks the best for others]."* (AMP emphasis added) It appears that love functions in a dual capacity. It constructs a shield or sets up a *fence* to keep out the offense or keep it from affecting us, while simultaneously concealing, shielding or fencing in the offender, so that their offense isn't observed by others, and overlooked by us. Love is *kind* to the unkind and *unselfish* to the selfish!

Canopy can be defined as "a protective covering." My first thought was that love covers with protection. A canopy is also defined as "a cover (as of cloth) fixed or carried above a person of high rank or a sacred object." This is my favorite, because it reminds me that we are *"God's chosen treasure – priests who are kings, a spiritual 'nation' set apart as God's devoted ones."* (1 Peter 2:9). Another definition for canopy is "an ornamental cloth covering hung or held up over something, especially a throne." This reminds me that Love or the canopy of love is beautiful, decorative, and it's attractive. When God occupies the throne of our hearts, we *overlook unkindness* and *disregard offenses* of others. This beauty is beheld by both, God and others.

As I considered love's capacity and commitment to covering, my attention was called to a portion of Scripture which reads, *"...love draws a veil over every insult and finds a way to make sin disappear."* (Proverbs 10:12 TPT) Because love is *"not self-seeking"* (see 1 Corinthians 13:5), the *loving individual* isn't insistent on covering up their own insults or offenses, or even acknowledging they were offended, and demand an apology. Instead, they are *intentional* in covering or providing a "veil" for the individual who intended to insult or offend *them*!

This is because the loving person is more concerned with *concealing* the matter, than *catching feelings* or getting an attitude. They understand that *"the prudent man ignores an insult."* (see Proverbs 12:16) They are also aware that it is advantageous and to *"his glory to overlook a transgression or an offense."* (see Proverbs 19:11) The individual demonstrating love, desires discretion over division, and unification over separation. They consider concealing the offense a priority, because they've learned that *"He who covers and forgives an offense seeks love, but he who repeats or harps on a matter separates even close friends."* (Proverbs 17:9)

During my studies, I discovered that canopy, in other languages, can mean "couch with mosquito curtains" (Greek), "mosquito net over bed" (Latin), and "mosquito or gnat curtain" (Egyptian). This interests me, for a few reasons. First, because gnats are small, but they can not only be a nuisance – but they can also be absolutely annoying or irritating. However, mosquitos are worse because they draw blood, carry disease, and spread viruses. I believe that love serves as a canopy or *curtain* to keep out the spiritual insects – gnats and mosquitos that intend to *irritate* and *infect* us. Suffering from too many mosquito bites can leave us and drained, weak and diseased – whether the insect bites occur in the natural or spiritual.

Love is not easily angered, irritated, or provoked – *"it is not touchy or fretful or resentful; it takes no account of the evil done to it [it pays no attention to a suffered wrong]."* (see 1 Corinthians 13:5) The Passion Translation reads, *"Love is not easily irritated or quick to take offense."* Love protects us from infectious pests or *insects* – whether they're physical ones or spiritual ones.

"Love bears up under anything and everything that comes, is ever ready to believe the best of every person, its hopes are <u>fadeless under all circumstances</u>, and it endures everything [without weakening]." (1 Corinthians 13:7 emphasis added) And those who love (*without weakening*) wear this covering – their canopy or curtain, not only as a *badge of honor*, but also as a *banner*!

Love Is Our Banner

In addition to love being a *close* covering, love is also a seemingly not-so-close covering. However, His love is closer than we can ever calculate. In reality, He (Love) lives *within us*! *"For we are the temple of the living God; even as God said, I will dwell in and with and among them and will walk in and with and among them, and I will be their God, and they shall be My people."* (2 Corinthians 6:16b) He also said, *"See! The abode of God is with men, and He will live (encamp, tent) among them; and they shall be His people,*

It's All We Can Eat!

and God shall personally be with them and be their God." (Revelation 21:3b) In order better explain the benefit of being under a banner, and give a greater example of its direct impact from a distance, let's look in the book of Exodus.

At this point in time, Moses was tasked with taking the children of Israel from the bondage of slavery in Egypt, and escorting them through the wilderness, to the *promised land*. At one point during this pilgrimage, they engaged in battle against the Amalekites. After prevailing against them, the Lord commanded Moses to commemorate the encounter, and preserve this point in time, by writing about it in a book and rehearsing *"in the ears of Joshua"* what He intended to do with their adversaries. This was Moses' response: *"And Moses built an altar and called the name of it, The Lord is my Banner;"* (Exodus 17:15). In some translations, it reads, *"...and called the name of it Jehovah-Nissi."*

The Hebrew word for *"Banner"* is *nes* (nace). It is defined as a "standard, ensign, signal, sign." It can also mean "flag, flagstaff" or "pole." It comes from the Hebrew word *nacac* (naw-sas), which can mean to sparkle or "to gleam from afar", "be conspicuous as a signal, to raise a beacon." More specifically, "a flag fluttering in the wind." In essence, a banner was a rallying or focal point. It was a signal and the place where armies would assemble themselves. It was a place – usually on a hill or high point (see Isaiah 18:3), to look to and be reminded of your identity and the people or cause for which you were fighting. In a sense, it was a source of inspiration and strength.

In order to get a better idea of the beauty and benefit of a banner, I'll have to go back, a little further in Exodus 17. When the time came for them to fight against the Amalekites, Moses told Joshua, *"Tomorrow I will stand on the top of the hill with the rod of God in my hand...and Moses, Aaron, and Hur went up to the <u>hilltop</u>. When Moses* *held up his hand, Israel prevailed; and when he lowered his hand, Amalek, prevailed. But Moses' hands were heavy and weary. So [the other men] took a stone and put it under him and he sat on it. Then Aaron and Hur held up his hands, one on one side and one on the other side; so his hands were steady until the going down of the sun. And Joshua mowed down and disabled Amalek and his people with the sword."* (see Exodus 17:9-13 emphasis added).

There are several points I'd like to make, pertaining to the Lord being our Banner, as well as the part we must play – our participation in being a banner in other people's battles and subsequent victories. I will begin by stating the obvious: throughout their wilderness journey, Jehovah demonstrated that He was their *Covering* and *Banner*, by appearing above and before them *"...by day in a pillar of cloud to lead them along the way and by night in a pillar of fire to give them light, that they might travel by day and by night."* (see Exodus 31:21) He was there, as their *Covering*, 24/7 (night and day). He is Love, and He does the same for us. He is with us 24/7, 365 (night and day, all year, every year) as our Ever-Present Help. As His children, having His same DNA, we are supposed to have the *same love* for others.

In the same way Jehovah-Nissi positioned Himself at the highest point, Moses positioned himself on the hilltop, where Joshua and the army would be able to see him holding up his staff, with his hands *stretched* towards the Lord, Jehovah-Nissi. One of the ways that we can demonstrate our love and that we are a covering, is to *prominently* position ourselves. We have to be *very present and easily visible*. We don't have to hold up a rod or staff, because the power of God (which the rod represented) resides within us.

Another thing that caught my attention, as being a *covering*, was the comfort and cooperation provided by *"the*

It's All We Can Eat!

other men." Aaron and Hur took a stone and set it under or behind Moses so he could be seated. Then each of them held up one of his arms, *"so his hands were steady."* They were not satisfied to sit there on the hilltop with Moses, as spectators. No, they *stood up, and stepped in*! They also remained *present and in position* until their army *prevailed*. One of the things that we can do to show love and cover, is by supporting, stabilizing, and lending our strength to those who are weak – we should bear *their* burden.

This is why we have such commands as: *"Carry one another's burdens and in this way you will fulfill the requirements of the law of Christ [that is, the law of Christian love]."* (Galatians 6:2 AMP) *"We then that are strong ought to bear the infirmities of the weak..."* (Romans 15:1 KJV) We should always remember that *"Love bears up under anything and everything that comes, is ever ready to believe the best of every person, its hopes are fadeless under all circumstances, and it endures everything [without weakening]. Love never fails [never fades out or becomes obsolete or comes to an end]."* (see 1 Corinthians 13:7-8a)

I had a thought that was not only interesting, but also inescapable. It was concerning the position of the banner or covering. It is always placed at the high point – the hilltop or mountaintop. In other words, the banner is always positioned at the pinnacle. Because it is positioned at the pinnacle, summit, or on a peak; those that are participating in battle can take a peek at the peak and be empowered to *persevere*! While writing this chapter, during my daily devotional time, I read, *"Revive us, O God! Let Your beaming face shine upon us with the sunrise rays of glory; then nothing will be able to stop us."* (Psalm 80:3 TPT emphasis added)

As I pondered upon the high position, and that some of the meanings for banner are a *beacon, sign, signal flagpole*; the Holy Spirit impressed upon me, a passage of Scripture. It reads, *"You are the light of [Christ to] the world. A city set on a hill cannot be hidden;"* (Matthew 5:14 AMP) The Passion Translation reads, *"Your lives light up the world. Let others see your light from a distance, for how can you hide a city that stands on a hilltop?"* (emphasis added) After sharing His observation, the Lord shows us *our obligation* in verse 16: *"Let it shine brightly before others, so that the commendable things you do will shine as light upon them..."*

I believe that one of the commendable things that we can do is show them love by both, *covering* them and *encouraging* them. By virtue of being *in Christ* (see Colossians 3:1), we are already raised to a *high point*, and therefore, are in their view. All we have to do is *shine* or as one of the meanings states *sparkle – be a beacon*!

The Beauty And Blessing of a Banner

In addition to a banner being a *sign* or *signal* for the soldiers to look to and be encouraged, it also served as a *standard* or rallying point. A standard is defined as a "distinguishing mark." It's a "warning." It appears that the banner had a dual purpose. It was a signal to strengthen the soldiers, and also a warning sign to stir up fear in the enemy armies. As I wrote this section, the Psalm that came to mind was *"God! Arise with awesome power, and every one of Your enemies will scatter in fear!"* (Psalm 68:1 TPT) I thought that this would be some sort of side note or secondary Scripture. However, that wasn't the case.

That's because prior to that Scripture passage being impressed upon me, the Holy Spirit had reminded me of Isaiah 59:19b, which reads, *"When the enemy shall come in like a flood, the Spirit of the Lord will lift up a standard against him and put him to flight [for He will come like a rushing stream which the breath of the Lord drives]."*

It's All We Can Eat!

(emphasis added) After reading this, I was curious about how other translations rendered this verse, and I was quite surprised, as I read the interpretation from The Message.

The Message reads, *"He dressed in Righteousness, put it on like a suit of armor, with Salvation on His head like a helmet, put on Judgment like an overcoat, and threw a cloak of Passion across His shoulders."* (Isaiah 59:16-17 MSG) Once again, I was reminded of the commentary of Colossians 3:14, that referred to previously, which stated, "Divine love is to be put on as the outer garment and finishing touch to a well-dressed Christian." This Scripture passage in Isaiah, from The Message, painted a picture for the me, of Love putting on love, getting dressed for battle, as my *Banner*, to fight for and rescue me! That's because Love *covers* us – He comes and *stands out* – He *shines* forth, as a *standard* and *signal* when we are engaged in warfare! We have the same responsibility, to be a banner – serve as standard, and come through, to cover our Brothers and Sisters in battle.

Banner Of Love

It is such a blessing to be covered and comforted by our *Banner*. He not only covers and comforts us, but He also escorts us into a place of *intimacy* and *exclusivity* with Him. In alluding to Him as the Bridegroom and us as His bride, it is written, *"He brought me into the banqueting house, and his banner over me was love [for love waved as a protecting and comforting banner over my head when I was near him]."* (Song of Solomon 2:4)

His covering, protection, and comfort are so great, that they can transport our minds from a battlefield to a banquet hall! It reminds me of Psalm 23a, where David wrote, *"You prepare a table for me in the presence of my enemies."* He was someone who knew all about the peace, comfort, and covering protection found in His Presence.

Nothing, nor no one was a threat to him (or us) when he was (and we are) *"near" Him*!

It's also a blessing to know that He not only covers and comforts us, but He also considers us *"beautiful"* and compares us to *"banners"*! He says that we're as beautiful and *"...as majestic as an army with billowing banners." "...awe-inspiring as an army with banners." "...like an army flying flags [awesome like an army under banners." "...as regal as an army beneath their banners."* (see Song of Solomon 6:4-10 NLT, HCSB, EXB, The Voice respectively)

Because we share His DNA, when we're walking in His will, we resemble Him – He sees His reflection in us, and He rejoices over us! In fact, we have the precious promise that *"The Lord your God is in the midst of you, a Mighty One, a Savior [Who saves]! He will rejoice over you with joy; He will rest [in silent satisfaction] and in His love [He will be silent and make no mention [of past sins, or even recall them]; He will exult over you with singing."* (Zephaniah 3:17) Did you see that?! Our Savior, Banner, and Strong Tower *sings* over us!

We are called to be a banner because our God is a Banner. *"Love is a safe place of shelter, for it never stops believing the best in others."* (1 Corinthians 13:7 TPT) We are to be a place where people can come and be sheltered. When people feel safe, even if they are sometimes insulting or offensive, they experience a freedom or liberty to be themselves, while they grow and mature in love. That's because love covers them – it believes *"the best in others"* – it becomes a banner over them, in their vulnerability, and they become liberated. Yes, love *liberates*!

It's "All We Can Eat!", Family. Let's Consistently Cover Others!

Chapter 6
Love Liberates!

"Love does not a traffic in shame and disrespect, nor selfishly seek its own honor. Love is not easily irritated or quick to take offense. Love joyfully celebrates honesty and finds no delight in what is wrong. Love is a safe place of shelter, for it never stops believing the best for others. Love never takes failure as defeat, for it never gives up."
(1 Corinthians 13:5-7 TPT)

Liberating Love

Access to our life of liberty begins with acknowledging and accepting our Heavenly Father's offer for adoption. *"For it was always his perfect plan to <u>adopt us as his delightful children</u>...so that his <u>tremendous love</u> that cascades over us would glorify his grace – for <u>the same love he has for his Beloved One, Jesus, he has for us</u>. And this unfolding plan brings him great pleasure!"* *"He <u>made us accepted</u> in the Beloved."* (see Ephesians 1:5-6 NKJV, TPT respectively, emphasis added)

We weren't an accident. We weren't a mistake. We weren't left on His Heavenly *doorstep*. This was His *planned* Parenthood! He *delighted* in adopting us. He *deliberately* liberated and delivered us! With His *purchasing power*, God was pleased to give His Son to rescue and redeem us – to be the *"propitiation for our sins."* (see 1 John 2:2) As our Advocate, *"He has rescued us completely..."* from the authority and rule of the adversary. *"[The Father] has delivered and drawn us to Himself out of the control and dominion of darkness and has transferred us into the kingdom of the Son of His love."* (Colossians 1:13)

Once we accepted Jesus Christ as our Lord and Savior, we were adopted into the family of God. This, in itself, is *powerful*! However, what actually happened is that we received *sonship*. Saint John wrote, *"But to as many as did receive and welcome Him, He gave the <u>authority</u> (<u>power, privilege, right</u>) to become the children [sons] of God, that is, to those who believe in (adhere to, trust in, and rely on) His name –"* (John 1:12 emphasis added) Our liberty is *laden* with power, rights, and privileges! *"Blessed be the Lord, Who daily loads us with benefits, The God of our salvation! Selah"* (Psalm 68:19 NKJV)

As it pertains to our privilege of sonship, the Apostle John also wrote, *"And see what [<u>an incredible</u>] <u>quality</u> of* *love the Father has given (shown, bestowed on) us, that we should be [permitted to] be named and called and counted the <u>children of God</u>! <u>And so we are</u>!"* (1 John 3:1a emphasis added) The Passion Translation reads, *"Look with wonder at <u>the depth</u> of the Father's <u>marvelous love</u> that He has <u>lavished on us</u>! He has called us and made us his very own beloved children."* (emphasis added)

I could go from A to Z in how He loves us. However, I will just stick to the previous paragraphs in describing His love for us. He loves us incredibly, deeply, definitely, marvelously, and lavishly. If this extravagant love were not enough, in addition to this quality or level of love, He also loves us *eternally*!

It is said of us, *"Yes! Look how you've made all your lovers to flourish like palm trees, each one growing in victory, standing with strength! You transplanted them into your heavenly courtyard, where they are thriving before you. For in your presence they will overflow and be anointed. Even in their old age they will stay fresh, bearing luscious fruit and abiding faithfully."* (Psalm 92:12-14 TPT) Verse 14 in The Amplified Classic reads, *"[Growing in grace] they shall still bring forth fruit in old age; they shall be full of sap [of spiritual vitality] and [rich and the] verdure [of trust, love, and contentment]."*

This level of love also has many fringe benefits. However, I believe a primary privilege – one that should not be considered only a fringe benefit, is our *freedom* or liberty. We're not on the fringe. We're right there, in His *"courtyard"* – privileged to be in His Presence, where we have the *freedom to flourish*! It is His love that is *developed* in us, that allows us to stand firm, strengthened, liberated, and safe from enslavement. However, this shield, shelter, security – this lifetime of liberty is a result of us *remaining* there.

In other words, as long as we remain *standing* in His Presence or remain in His love, we will remain *liberated* or kept free from slavery! We are instructed, *"In [this] freedom Christ has made us free [and completely liberated us]; stand fast then, and do not be hampered and held ensnared and submit again to a yoke of slavery [which you have once put off]."* (Galatians 5:1) His love for us liberates us, and *our love for Him* keeps us liberated!

True Love/Truly In Love

Explaining our Heavenly Father's eternal love, The Lord Jesus said, *"Now a slave does not remain in the household permanently (forever); the son [of the house] does remain forever. So if the Son liberates you [makes you free men], then you are really an unquestionably free."* This proceeded the promise, *"...If you abide in My word [hold fast to My teachings and live in accordance with them], you are truly My disciples. And you will know the Truth, and the Truth will set you free."* (see John 8:31-36) Knowing the Truth, not only sets or makes us free, it also makes us *fruitful* – it sets us up to *flourish*!

In those days, a slave couldn't remain in the household forever. I guess you could say that the house was not big enough for the son and the slave. Maybe it was not so much the size of the *house*, but the size of the father's heart – his attention and affection. However, there's *plenty of room* in our Heavenly Father's household, and His heart! Because of His extravagant love for us, His evaluation of us is not as servants or slaves. Instead, He esteems us as sons – extending to us the *same love* as He extended to His Son and our Savior, Jesus Christ! He said, *"There's more than enough room in My Father's home..."* (John 14:2 NLT)

The Greek word used for *"liberate"* is *eleuthero* (el-yoo-ther-o-o). It means "to exempt from liability, deliver from obligation" and "to release from bondage." Because the Son has set us free – liberated us, we now live a life *unrestricted* by sin, *unshackled* from shame, and *unrestrained* by darkness. We're now, no longer living *restricted*, *shackled*, and *restrained*, because we were delivered into the Kingdom of Light and Truth.

The key to our liberty and release from bondage, is our knowledge – our experiential awareness or recognition of our Redeemer, and our perception of Him is predicated on us abiding in His word and us remaining or loving and living in it. This is why He later said, *"If you [really] love Me, you will keep (obey) My commands." "Loving me empowers you to obey my commands."* (John 14:15 AMPC, TPT respectively)

In a previous chapter, I mentioned a commentary of Colossians 3:14, which stated, "Divine love is to be put on as the outer garment and finishing touch to a well-dressed Christian." It was also noted, "…one is to put on this outer cloak as the bond of perfectness or as a girdle. It is to cover all, unite all, and bind all together as one. This is true perfection." I refer to this because I was reminded that when describing the full armor of God, the *first* thing that we are told to put on is the *"girdle"* or *"belt of truth."*

We are instructed, *"Stand therefore [hold your ground], having tightened the belt of truth around your loins and having put on the breastplate of integrity and of moral rectitude and right standing with God,"* (Ephesians 6:14) The Passion Translation begins, *"Put on truth as a belt to strengthen you to stand in triumph."* A few things that I learned from this passage is that truth provides strength and stability and helps us keep things together. Also, truth, integrity, and righteousness are essential to standing our ground and being victorious, when it comes to spiritual warfare.

If you have never done a study on the whole armor of God or in this case, *"the belt of truth"* you're in for a surprise. For example, the belt of the truth was sort of like a utility belt or harness. It was the first piece of armor or equipment that the Roman soldier would put on, and on which other pieces of his armor would somehow, attach or be connected. For instance, the piece of equipment that held his sword in place, as well as the protective leather strips that hung from his waist, were attached to the belt or harness.

As it pertains to our topic of love, it is impossible to operate in love, without being securely held together in truth, stabilized by integrity, and protected by righteousness. This is how we are able engage in warfare, as soldiers and stand victorious. We should never forget that we are warriors – that we're waging war to liberate others, while maintaining our own liberty, and that we (when operating in love) are *"more than conquers"* (see Romans 8:37).

This is so appropriate, as it pertains to love, because love rejoices in the truth – *"rejoices when right and truth prevail"* (see 1 Corinthians 13:6). The Message reads, *"Takes pleasure in the flowering of truth."* In my next volume in the series – Joy, I write about it in more detail. However for now, I will write that rejoicing, and finding joy in what is the truth and what is right, is a *strategy*!

Think About Love

In order to rejoice in what is the truth and what is right, we must first *think* about them. In case you're wondering what the results are, when we choose to think about and rejoice in what is right and what is true, the Apostle Paul wrote: *"Rejoice in the Lord always [delight, take pleasure in Him]; again I will say, rejoice! And the peace of God [that peace which reassures the heart, that peace] which transcends all understanding, [that peace which] stands guard over your hearts and your minds in*

Christ Jesus [is yours]. Finally, believers, <u>whatever is true</u>, whatever is honorable and worthy of respect, <u>whatever is right</u> and confirmed by God's word, whatever is pure and wholesome, whatever is lovely and brings peace…<u>think continually on these things [center your mind on them and implant them in your heart]</u> …and the God [who is the source] of peace and well-being <u>will be with you</u>." (Philippians 4:4, 7-9 AMP emphasis added)

One of the first keys that I saw when reading this is that we must *"rejoice in the Lord always."* As a result, God's peace will position itself over our *"hearts and minds."* A warrior and worshipper who worked this strategy very well, was King David. He declared, *"I will bless the Lord in all times; His praise shall continually be in my mouth. My soul makes its boast in the Lord; The humble and downtrodden will hear it and rejoice."* (Psalm 34:1-2 AMP) He knew that if he continually thought about, rejoiced in, and praised God, God would inhabit his praises, and God's peace would accompany or be present with Him, in King David's praise. When He shows up, everything we need, shows up *with* Him. That's because *He* is All we need!

Besides King David's proficiency at praising God continually, the Prophet Isaiah provides this promise: *"You will guard him and keep him in perfect and constant peace whose mind [both inclination and its character], is stayed on You, because he commits himself to You, leans on You, and hopes confidently in You."* (Isaiah 26:3) When we commit to confidently and constantly thinking on and trusting in God – fixed and focused on Christ (Truth), we are not only blessed in getting an angel or a bodyguard; we get and are *kept* by God's peace!

In addition to fixing our focus on Christ, we are also commanded to focus on a combination other concerns. Included in this list of concerns, we are charged to think continually on *"whatever is true"* and *"whatever is right."* When we do so, we can be assured and comforted in knowing *"the God [who is the source] of peace and well-being will be with you."* When we operate in what is true and what is right, The One Who is *"Faithful and True"* will occupy the area *with* us!

Whatever is true and right are great items to give attention to. However, we must go further in our thinking and knowledge. We must also think on what is true and right about *ourselves* and about *others*. Not only must we think on *what* is true and right about ourselves and about others, we must also know *Who* is True or *The Truth* and *Right*! What is written about *The Truth* is, *"And righteousness shall be the girdle of His waist and faithfulness girdle of his loins."* (Isaiah 11:5) *"...The One Who was riding it is called Faithful (Trustworthy, Loyal, Incorruptible, Steady) and True..."* (see Revelation 19:11)

In order to love with His level or quality of love, we must *know* – be intimate with The Truth. When we do, we will know *how* to love. One thing that we must know about Him is that He is The Truth Who *liberates* or *sets us free*. He said, *"The Spirit of the Lord is upon Me (the Messiah), Because He has anointed Me...He has sent Me to announce release (pardon, forgiveness) to the captives, And recovery of sight to the blind, To set free those who are oppressed (downtrodden, bruised, crushed, by tragedy),"* (see Luke 4:18) He proclaimed – publicly and persuasively preached and made everyone who heard what was heralded accountable. That's because *"...faith comes by hearing [what is told], and what is heard comes by the preaching [of the message that came from the lips] of Christ (the Messiah Himself)."* (Romans 10:17)

He didn't have to turnover tables, throw a temper tantrum, overthrow the government, incite a riot, or start a

It's All We Can Eat!

war. He simply *spoke* the Word of Truth. As a result, many have experienced rescue, liberty, healing, deliverance, and wholeness. We have a reminder of this revelation in Psalms, where it is written, *"He sends forth His word and heals them and rescues them from the pit and destruction."* (Psalm 107:20) This is *Liberating* Love!

Let Your Love Light And Love Life Shine!

He is *"the Way, and the Truth, and the Life..."* (see John 14:6) Until we adequately and intimately *know* Him – our Truth, we will remain blind, in prison, unpardoned, unforgiven, captive, bruised, and crushed. I met someone a couple of years ago, who was very bitter. She often complained about things that had been done to her, and would often finish her sentences with "this is my truth." I was sensing that some other things were going on with her, or had taken place. In fact, my discernment was showing me that she was dealing with self-deception, rejection, and some other issues. Then the Holy Spirit said to me, "Don't make their 'truth' your truth if it isn't *The* Truth!" Otherwise, I could end up in a similar cell, serving a self-imposed sentence, unable to be set free!

If we're not careful, cognizant of, and committed to The Truth, other people's bondage can become *our* bondage – leaving us in need of being set free! When we embrace *their* truth, we may eventually experience their tragedies. So much of our success, deliverance, and salvation is dependent upon our spiritual discernment and knowledge of The Truth. We are advised, *"...through knowledge and superior discernment shall the righteous be delivered."* (see Proverbs 11:9) *"...revelation knowledge will rescue the righteous."* (TPT) However, we can't be satisfied or become complacent with our own success and deliverance. Our Redeemer and Rescuer requires more from us. We have other responsibilities. We're responsible for reaching and restoring others. The same spiritual discernment and revelation knowledge that rescues us, can be used to even save a city! Verse ten reads, *"The blessing that rests on the righteous releases strength and favor to the entire city."*

We have a responsibility to facilitate the release, rescue or recovery of our brothers and sisters. We are informed to use our influence as an instrument to instill hope (Proverbs 11:11). This is why the Lord said to Simon Peter, *"and when you yourself have returned to Me, strengthen your brethren."* (Luke 22:32 NKJV) The Passion Translation reads, *"after you have turned back to me and have been restored, make it your life mission to strengthen the faith of your brothers."* (emphasis added) The word used for "strengthen" means to "firmly establish, give support to, to secure or firmly plant in such a way, that it eliminates vacillation."

In order for us to eliminate their vacillation, we must be instrumental in restoring their vision. We do this by introducing or exposing them to the *"Life"* and the *"Light"* – Jesus Christ, Himself. *"In Him was Life, and the Life was the Light of men. And the Light shines on in the darkness, for the darkness has never overpowered it [put it out or absorbed it or appropriated it, and is unreceptive to it]."* In the same way that Elisha prayed, *"Lord, I pray You, open his eyes that he may see."* (see 2 Kings 6:17), we must pray, "Lord, open their eyes, so that they see You, and that You love them."

It is our responsibility to reveal Divinity to humanity. By introducing or exposing them to the Light and Life, the Light and Life has the opportunity to enter their life. Then, they can see that Divinity has light and love or a *heart* for humanity, *"...for his life is the light for all humanity."* (John 1:4b TPT) This is a lovely opportunity for a "light bulb" moment! Once they perceive His Presence, it will shine *light* on, and speak *life* to them! They will see and discern this, because it is written, *"The entrance and unfolding of Your words give light; their unfolding gives understanding (discernment and comprehension) to the simple."* (Psalm 119:130)

The Passion Translation reads, *"Break open your word within me until revelation-light shines out! Those with open hearts are given insight into your plans."* He is The Bread of Life (see John 6:35). In the same way that He took the bread, gave thanks, blessed it, broke it, and then gave it to the disciples to feed the multitude (see Matthew 14:13-21), He also wants to break the bread, bless it, and give it to us to be fed, as well as for us give it to others to eat. As we feed them, they will be able to feed others. Exposing or introducing others to the Light and Life is intrinsic to our life's mission.

In this same way that we were instructed, *"…make it your life mission to strengthen the faith of your brothers."* (see Luke 22:32), and also, how the Lord informed His parents, *"…I must be about My Father's business"* (see Luke 2:49); we must make sure that we're on our *mission* and about our Father's *business*! In other words, "We've got to be *about that Life!*" That mission, business, and being *about that life* or as some might say, "being 'bout it – 'bout it" is to *"[Strive to] save others, snatching [them] out of [the] fire;"* (see Jude 1:23)

Here's a synopsis of a historical figure and Biblical hero – a *First Responder* who knew how to *be about his father's business*. This is how David described the daring rescue: *"And David said to Saul, Your servant kept <u>his father's sheep</u>. And when there came the lion or again a bear and took a lamb out of the flock, <u>I went out after it</u> and smote it <u>and delivered the lamb out of its mouth</u>; and when it arose against me, I caught it by its beard and smote it and killed*

It's All We Can Eat!

it." (1 Samuel 17:34-35 emphasis added) Because he was in the habit of delivering or snatching his father's sheep – rescuing and liberating the lambs, he was confident that God would be with him to deliver Israel from those that defied God – from the jaws of Goliath and his army!

In the same way that David rescued – snatched the sheep from the lion's mouth, we must be ready to snatch others *from the fire*. We may not be able to extinguish the flames, but we can certainly illuminate the escape route. God provides *"a way of escape"* (see 1 Corinthians 10:13), and sometimes we are the ones who usher them (our Father's sheep) to The Way (Christ). The Lord expects us to light the way to *The Way* (see John 14:6)! We are encouraged, *"but the people who know their God shall be strong, and carry out great exploits [for God]"* (Daniel 11:32b NKJV) Escorting others to the *"way of escape"* and rescuing the Father's sheep are *great exploits*!

We are called or assigned as *First Responders*! We're in the *rescue and recovery* business. The Greek word for *"snatch"* is *harpazo* (har-pad-zo). It can mean "to catch up, carry off, confiscate, pluck, plunder, pull" and "snatch away." More specifically, it means "to seize by force, snatch up suddenly and decisively." However, the seizure is not executed secretly. Instead, it is defined as "to take by an open display of force." This reminds me of Colossians 2:15, which reads, *"[God] disarmed the principalities and powers that were ranged against us and made a bold display and public example of them, in triumphing over them in Him and in it [the cross]."* (emphasis added) We too, are commissioned to execute spiritual *search and seizures*!

The Greek word for *"save"* is *sozo* (sode-zo). It can mean "to deliver, heal, preserve, protect, rescue" and "be (make) whole." A more accurate description is "to deliver out of danger and into safety." More specifically, it speaks of "God rescuing believers from the penalty and power of sin, and into His provisions (safety)." The proper word to use is *soterion* (so-tay-ree-on), which means "saved/rescued from destruction and brought into divine safety."

It has always been God's desire to deliver us. Some examples are when He said, *"...you were as a brand plucked out of the burning..."* (Amos 4:11), and *"...is not this [returned captive Joshua] the brand plucked out of the fire?"* (Zechariah 3:2b) Because we have been delivered, plucked, and rescued, our appropriate response is to be First Responders – be *about that Life* and *be about* our *"Father's business!"*

Some may ask, "But how do we do this? How can we 'Be about *that* Life!?'" My reply is, "By releasing or *speaking The Word*." We are encouraged, *"So, go ahead – let <u>everyone know it!</u> <u>Tell the world how he broke through and delivered you from the power of darkness</u> and has gathered us together from all over the world. <u>He has set us free to be his very own</u>!* (Psalm 107:2-3 TPT) When we release or speak The Word, we release and speak Life (Christ), Who can release and rescue those who are imprisoned. If we want to break down prison walls, break up binding chains, and bust open enslaving shackles, we're going to have to give our testimony – we're going to have to tell others how He delivered *us*!

We were once alienated, isolated, estranged, and separated. With a *liberating love* far more superior to any lottery ticket, He set us free! Not only did He set us free, but He has also reconciled us to Himself (see Colossians 1:21-22)! Therefore, with the same excitement with which we would proclaim a job promotion or marriage proposal, we should pronounce our *release from prison and reconciliation* with God!

It's All We Can Eat!

Some of us once sat in darkness, living in the dark shadows of death. <u>We were prisoners to our pain, chained to our regrets</u>. Our own pain became our punishment. ...Then we cried out, "Lord, help us! Rescue us!" And he did! <u>His light broke through the darkness, and he led us out in freedom from death's dark shadow and snapped every one of our chains</u>. ...For he smashed through heavy prison doors and shattered the steel bars that held us back, <u>just to set us free!</u>" (see Psalm 107:10-16 TPT emphasis added) Now, THAT'S *Liberating Love!*

Once upon a time, we were *"once like corpses"* caught up in and directed by *"the deeds and desires of our self-life. We lived by whatever natural cravings and thoughts our minds dictated..."* We, without any help, rights, or hope, *"once lived and conducted ourselves in the passions of our flesh [our behavior governed by our corrupt and sensual nature], obeying the impulses of the flesh and the thoughts of the mind [our cravings dictated by our senses and our dark imaginings]."* (see Ephesians 2:1-3 TPT, AMPC respectively) I've never watched the popular TV show, but I get the sense that spiritually, we were like some of the characters in "The Walking Dead." However, *The Resurrection* and *The Life* (see John 11:25) – our Redeemer, Reconciler, and Restorer stepped in and *released* us! THIS is *Liberating Love*!

"Even when <u>we were dead (slain) by [our own] shortcomings</u> and trespasses, <u>He made us alive</u> together in fellowship and in union with Christ; [<u>He gave us the very life of Christ Himself</u>, <u>the same new life</u> with which He quickened Him, for] it is by grace (His favor and mercy which you did not deserve) that you're saved (delivered from judgment and made partakers of Christ's salvation)." (Ephesians 2:5 emphasis added)

It's All We Can Eat!

Those passages of Scripture from Psalm 107 reminded me of another passage, concerning others who were in in darkness and despair, in need of deliverance, and relying on God to rescue them, *and He did*! It also illustrates two other ways that we can "be about that life" – *prayer* and *praise*. It reads, "*...It was so bad we didn't think we were going to make it. <u>We felt like we'd been sent to death row</u>, that it was all over for us...we were forced to trust God totally—not a bad idea since <u>he's the God who raises the dead</u>! <u>And he did it</u>, <u>rescued us from certain doom</u>. And he'll do it again, <u>rescuing us as many times as we need rescuing</u>. <u>You and your prayers are part of the rescue operation</u>—I don't want you in the dark about that either. I can see your faces even now, lifted <u>in praise for God's deliverance</u> of us, a <u>rescue in which your prayers played such a crucial part</u>.*" (see 2 Corinthians 1:8-11 MSG emphasis added)

Since the shackles were shattered, the chains were snapped, and we have been drawn out of death's darkness, into liberty with the with the *same* Light, Love, and Life of Christ; we should *shine brightly* – sharing with others, what He has done for us, *and what He will do for them*! This is neither a recommendation, nor just an encouragement, or suggestion; it's more like a command from God. The Psalmist wrote, *"Let everyone everywhere <u>shine with praise</u> to Yahweh! Let it all out! Go ahead and <u>praise him</u>!"* (Psalm 117:1 TPT)

By shining our *Love* light, we open up awesome opportunities to bring or point them to where they can openly offer up praise to Him, by proclaiming, *"Lord, because I am your loving servant, <u>you have broken open my life and freed me from my chains</u>."* (Psalm 116:16 TPT)

*"Out of my deep anguish and pain I prayed, and God, you helped me as a father. <u>You came to my rescue and broke open the way</u> into a beautiful and broad place. Now I

know, Lord, that <u>you are for me</u>, and I will never fear what man can do to me. For <u>you stand beside me as my hero who rescues me</u>." (Psalm 118:5-7b TPT) That's how we show and share *Liberating Love* – we shine our light!

"Here's another way to put it: You're here to be light...God is not a secret to be kept..." (see Matthew 5:14 MSG) As I alluded to earlier, we are *obligated and ordered* to light the way to *The Way* (Christ)! *"<u>Your lives light up the world</u>. <u>Let others see your light from a distance</u>, for how can you hide a city that stands on a hilltop? And who would light a lamp and then hide it in an obscure place? Instead, it's placed where everyone in the house <u>can benefit from its light</u>. So don't hide your light! <u>Let it shine brightly before others</u>, so that the commendable things you do will <u>shine as light upon them</u>..."* (Matthew 5:14-16 TPT emphasis added)

We were ordained and called to *occupy* – not to obscurity or complacency! We're not engaged in a covert operation. Instead, we are ordered to operate out, in the open, where everyone around us will *benefit*. When I read, *"a city set on a hill"* I think of another city that sat on a hill or mountain – Mount Zion, the city where God lives (see Psalms 48, 132).

What I learned recently, from reading the book *I Am Zion*, by Apostle John Eckhardt, is that *we*, as Believers – children of God, are Mt. Zion! Yes, we're that *"city on a hill"* and He chose us, lives in us, and *lights* us! He said, *"I will make this place my eternal dwelling, for I have loved and desired it as my very own!"* (see Psalm 132:13-14 TPT), and *"I will also <u>give you for a light to the nations</u>, that My salvation may extend to the ends of the earth."* (Isaiah 49:6 emphasis added) In the same way He occupies space in our hearts, He expects us to *occupy our space* – our sphere of influence on Earth!

It's All We Can Eat!

Immediately after talking to Zacchaeus, the tax collector in his home, the Lord taught the disciples a parable. Personally, I'd consider it a command. Within this parable is a principle which is imperative that we practice, if we are serious about *letting our light shine* and doing *"good works, which God prepared beforehand, that we should walk in them."* (see Ephesians 2:10) After announcing that *salvation* had come to the house of Zacchaeus, the Lord shared with them the story of a noble man. He said, *"And he called his ten servants, and delivered them ten pounds, and said unto them, Occupy until I come."* (Luke 19:13 KJV) Some translations read, *"Invest this for me..."* (NLT), *"Engage in business..."* (ESV), *"Conduct business..."* (BSB), *"Operate..."* (MSG), and *"Trade..."* (DBT).

The Greek word for *"occupy"* is *pragmateuomai* (prag-mat-yoo-om-ahee). It means "to busy oneself." Basically, it means "to do business." It can also mean "turning something over, manage profitably the capital at your disposal" and my *favorite*: (figuratively) "to bear much fruit." As I consider the definitions and descriptions, I can't help asking myself; "What's His ROI – what's His *return on investment* from me? How am I *occupying* the space He has given me? Exactly how *engaged* am I? Am I conducting the *business* that He commissioned? Does how I *operate* provoke people to praise and glorify God – does it appeal to them in such a way, that it prompts them to *want* what I have?

We can't say that we don't have something to invest, trade, or work with, because the same way the noble man gave his servants what he had, for them to conduct business; Christ, our Master, has given us what the *He* has! His Love is the *capital* – the *currency* with which we are to *occupy until He comes*. It is stored in a place where no one can steal it. *"For where your treasure is, there will your heart [your* wishes, your desires; that on which your life centers] will be also." (Matthew 6:21 AMP)

The Lord is our Light and our Salvation (see Psalm 27:1). After He proclaimed, *"Today is [Messianic and spiritual] salvation come to [all the members of] this household, since Zacchaeus too is a [real spiritual] son of Abraham;"* He proceeded to say, *"For the Son of Man came to seek and to save that which was lost."* (Luke 19:9-10) We are also called or have come to do the same – to be the light, letting it shine, and leading them to their Salvation, as we seek to save the lost from the flames, until He comes back; whether they're on the fringe, or *in the fire*!

Statute of Liberty

"Now the Lord is the Spirit, and where the Spirit of the Lord is, there is liberty (emancipation from bondage, true freedom)." (2 Corinthians 3:17 AMP) In other words, where The Holy Spirit is, there's the fruit of the Spirit, and *where the fruit of the Spirit* is, there is *liberty*! When we live in this *"liberty"* I believe in some ways, it could be considered obeying the law – *"the law of liberty [the moral instruction given by Christ, especially about love]."* (see James 1:25, 2:12b). Although I'll cover it in a later chapter of this volume, I'll insert right here, *"Against such things there is no law [that can bring a charge]."* (Galatians 5:23b) In other words, *this* law has no statute of *limitations*!

This liberty is the result of knowing *The Truth*. Where there is The Truth, there is liberty, and where there is liberty, there is *Love*. When we know Love, because we are remaining in Him, and because we are loved; we know the truth about Who He Is, and we also know the truth about *who we are in Him*! Therefore, we know what to pray for (what to ask for) – knowing that we can *"ask whatever you will, and it shall be done for you."* (see John 15:7) This is what I call *the fruit of liberty* – freedom to walk in *fullness of joy*, and live a life of *fruitfulness*.

The Greek word used for *"truth"* is *aletheia* (al-ay-thi-a). The proper definition is "reality." It also means "divine truth revealed to man." What the Lord wants, is for us know the *reality* of Who He is, who we are, and what we have in Him, instead of being bound by deceit and enslaved by illusions. He can make such declarations, place such demands, and expect us to respond to what He desires; because as Lord, He is Master – our *Authority* and *Owner*, with the absolute *right* to expect us to embrace such *realities*!

Truth is from the Old English word, *triewo*. It means "faith, faithfulness, fidelity, loyalty; veracity" and "covenant." Of course, as Believers, we know that the personification of fidelity and covenant is The One Who is *"Faithful and True"* (see Revelation 19:11), Jesus Christ.

The Greek word used for *"liberty"* is eleutheria (el-yoo-ther-ee-ah). It can mean "delivered, exempt" and "unrestrained." More specifically, it means "freedom from the dominion of corrupt desires, so that we do by the free impulse of the soul what the will of God requires." It's important I insert here, that we must remember that although He *"began a good work"* in us, and He is *"at work in"* us; He is not set on Autopilot. We must give Him *access* and *authority* to do the work through us – *"to will and to work for His good pleasure and satisfaction and delight"* (see Philippians 1:6; 2:13, and 1 Thessalonians 2:13 respectively). In return, He gives us *power and authority*. What an awesome exchange!

It's a matter of deciding what ship we want to sail through life on – the slave ship, or *sonship* – the original *Love* Boat! It requires that we reject one and *receive* the other, and there is plenty of room *for as many as would like* to sail! *"But to as many as did receive and welcome Him, He gave the authority (power, privilege, right) to become the children of God, that is, to those who believe in (adhere to, trust in, and rely on) His name."* (John 1:12) When He has access to us, through our submission, we escape enslavement and experience supernatural sonship.

In his letter to the church at Galatia (and us), the Apostle Paul encouraged, *"So, brethren, we [who are born again] are not children of a slave woman [the natural], but of the free [the supernatural]. In [this] freedom Christ has made us free [and completely liberated us]; stand fast then, and not be hampered and held ensnared and submit again to a yoke of slavery [which you have once put off]."* (Galatians 4:31-5:1) The Passion Translation of 4:31 reads, *"...we're the supernatural sons of the free woman - sons of grace!"*

Now that we've stepped up into our status of *supernatural sons and daughters of grace*, we must never become complacent with, or distracted by our status, and forget that *the purpose for such power is to serve others*! The *Apostle* Paul continued his encouragement to the church at Galatia (and us), *"For you, brethren, were [indeed] <u>called to freedom</u>; only [do not let your] freedom be an incentive to your flesh and an opportunity or excuse [for selfishness], <u>but through love you should serve one another</u>."* (Galatians 5:13 emphasis added)

The Weymouth New Testament reads, *"...but become bondservants to one another in a spirit of love."* The Greek word for bondservant is *doulos* (doo-los). According to Strong's, it means "someone who belongs to another; a bond-slave, without any rights of their own." However, bond-slave "is used with the highest dignity in the NT – namely, of believers who *willingly* live under Christ's authority as His devoted followers." You might say that we're His Love slaves, just as He is The Love Slave of The Father.

Eternal Love

In addition to this authority, we receive another powerful Gift. We received the Holy Spirit and His gifts. When I was adopted, no one told me that this would also *automatically* launch me into a leadership role. What I have since learned, is that every Believer is a Leader – even if the only one we're leading is ourselves. Concerning leadership qualities, as it pertains to the fruit of the Spirit; Author, Speaker, and Leadership Expert, John C. Maxwell writes, "Every leader should embrace this marvelous list of inward qualities. Evaluate yourself against them: Love: Is my leadership motivated by love for people?"

Love for people is indicative of the quality of life we live, or lack thereof. It speaks to whether we are *spiritually* alive or dead. Here is further evidence: *"We know that we have passed over out of death into Life by the fact that we love the brethren (our fellow Christians). He who does not love abides (remains, is held and kept continually) in [spiritual] death."* (1 John 3:14)

John's premise of what proves that we have passed from death to Life, is based on the Lord's promise, *"I assure you, most solemnly I tell you, the person whose ears are open to My words [who listens to My message] and believes and trusts in and clings to and relies on Him Who sent Me has (possesses now) eternal life…he has already passed over out of death into eternal life."* (see John 5:24)

"By this we know [and have come to understand the depth and essence of His precious] love: that He [willingly] laid down His life for us [because He loved us]. And we ought to lay down our lives for the believers." (1 John 3:16 AMP) One translator writes that when Jesus *"laid down His*

life for us" He in essence, "placed His soul over us and we are constantly indebted to place our souls over our brothers and sisters." This is that *fervent love* that I wrote about previously – that love that *covers, extends, stretches*! When we love like this – loving others, we are really *living*!

"Little children, let us not love [merely] in theory or in speech <u>but in deed and in truth</u> (in practice and in sincerity). By this we shall come to know (perceive, recognize, and understand) <u>that we are of the Truth</u>, and can reassure (quiet, conciliate, and pacify) our hearts in His presence," (1 John 3:18-19 emphasis added).

What we produce – the fruitfulness through our loving deeds, as a result of the fruit of the Spirit working in and through us, can and will win souls. This should be our goal since it brings glory to God. Here's the prophetic word from Proverbs 11:30: *"What good people produce is like a life-giving tree. Those who are wise give new life to others."* (ERV) *"Live right, and you will eat from the life-giving tree. And if you act wisely, others will follow."* (CEV), *"A good person gives life to others [the fruit of the righteous is the tree of life]; the wise person teaches others how to live [gathers lives/souls]."* (EXB), *"The fruit of the [uncompromisingly] righteous is a tree of life, and he who is wise captures human lives [for God, as a fisher of men – he gathers and receives them for eternity]."* (AMPC)

It's "All We Can Eat!", Family. Let's Let Our Love Light And Love Life Shine!

Chapter 7
Love Makes Things Happen!

"Everything we could ever need for life and godliness has already been deposited in us by his divine power. For all this was lavished upon us through the rich experience of knowing him who has called us by name and invited us to come to him
through a glorious manifestation of his goodness."
(2 Peter 1:3 TPT)

It's All We Can Eat!

I'll begin this chapter with a comment that may seem controversial to some readers. That statement is that *faith is not enough.* Similarly, *knowledge* is not enough, either! In other words, in the same way that faith by itself, is insufficient; knowledge in and of itself, is insufficient, as well. Some people erroneously embrace the idea that "knowledge is power." However, that is not true. Knowing is *not* enough. It is *understanding what to do with* that knowledge or *wisdom – how to apply the knowledge* in a way that is *advantageous* to us, that produces *power*!

This is why we were commanded, *"The beginning of Wisdom is: get Wisdom (skillful and godly wisdom)! [For skillful and godly Wisdom is the principal thing.] And with all you have gotten, get understanding (discernment, comprehension, and interpretation)."* (Proverbs 4:7) As you can see, *knowledge* isn't even noted! Therefore, we should not become content or complacent with just having knowledge. Instead, we should *prize* wisdom and understanding as *principal things* that *position* us for power! In the same sense, our faith is a *"principal thing."*

Faith is the *foundation* or principal thing, on which we must build or *add to*. This is fundamental in our lives being formed, us moving forward, and us becoming *fruitful*. We can do this because *deposited* in each us, was *"the degree of faith apportioned by God..."* (Romans 12:3) Other translations read, *"...your God-given faith as a standard of measurement..."* (TPT), and *"the measure of faith."* (KJV)

The Greek word used for *"measure"* is *metron* (met-ron). It means "an instrument for measuring, a vessel for receiving and determining the quantity of things." It is also defined as "determined extent, portion measured off, the standard for determining what is enough (or not enough)" and "the controlling basis by which something is determined as acceptable or unacceptable."

Webster's dictionary defines it as, "the extent, dimensions, capacity, etc. of anything, especially as determined by a standard." I couldn't help wondering, "Is this where we get the words meter and metered from?" However, I chose not to investigate. Because our measure our faith was deposited in, dispensed, or distributed to us, by Christ (see Ephesians 4:7); we are *never* operating at a deficit. He predetermined the extent or capacity we needed to do what He called us to do, and He *expects us to expand* or enlarge that capacity through our *exercising* or adding to that dimension.

I think of or compare our *"measure of faith"* to our muscular system, at birth. We were never given new muscles or a new muscular system. We have the same muscles and system that was predetermined *before* our birth. The reason that they look different now, than they did at birth, and how they look when we peek into a photo album at old pictures of us; is because they have *grown and developed* as a result of us *using and exercising* them! The term used in Hebrews 5:14 is *"...by reason of use..."* (KJV)

The principle that governs the growth and development of our physical muscles is the same principle that governs the growth and development of our faith or *faith muscles*. That principle is use or *exercise*. The Apostle Paul pointed out to his protégé Timothy, the profitability of training and exercise, and emphasized that the *spiritual* exercise was *more profitable* or *precious*. He wrote, *"For physical training is of some value (useful for a little), <u>but godliness (spiritual training) is useful and of value in everyday and in every way,</u> for it holds <u>promise for the present life</u> and also for the life which is to come."* (1 Timothy 4:8 emphasis added)

In other words, a sexy six-pack, a chiseled chest, and bulging biceps can only get us *so far*. They're fine, if we spend most of our time on the beach, in bodybuilding contests, or at photo shoots! But they can't help us successfully engage in *spiritual warfare*, live lives of *godliness*, serve others, and *glorify*, as well as *satisfy* God's requirements of us! We must prefer and prize what's precious! One thing that makes it precious and profitable is that it holds *"promise"* for our present and future lives. Of course, this is predicated upon us practicing – exercising, or *adding to* our spiritual gifts and fruit!

The Apostle Peter penned, *"...He has bestowed on us His precious and exceedingly great promises..."* (see 2 Peter 1:4) One such promise is what can be produced in the present and in the future, if we *exercise* and *add to* the measure of faith that was given to us. This preordained measure of faith is prerequisite for growth and building. Not only is it prerequisite to growth and building – it is *precious*! This word *"precious"* means that it should not only be viewed as *of value, honored, weighty* and *very costly* to us, but primarily, because it is viewed as weighty and *"precious"* by The One Who *provided* the promises!

Have you ever heard the phrase, "Move it, or lose it!"? Well, I saw this adage in action, or more accurately, during *inaction*. I used to work at a nursing home, years ago. Of the many conditions, ailments, and maladies that I learned about, the one that sticks out most, is atrophy. Atrophy is a wasting away through lack of nourishment, or a gradual decline of effectiveness or vigor, <u>especially due to underuse or neglect</u>.

Because of illness or injury, and possibly lack of use; some patients had limbs that had atrophied. In some cases, the nurses or nursing assistants would perform some sort of physical therapy, in hopes of restoring motion and use, or to

It's All We Can Eat!

avoid atrophy from setting in. As it applies to us, we must avoid *spiritual atrophy*, by refusing to remain motionless. We must *exercise* our gifts. We can't allow the gifts and abilities He's given us to be neutralized and *neglected*!

The Apostle Paul told Timothy (and us), *"Do not neglect the gift which is in you, [that special inward endowment] which was directly imparted to you [by the Holy Spirit] ..."* (1 Timothy 4:14) Some other translations read, *"Don't minimize the powerful gift that operates in your life..."* (TPT) *"Do not be careless about the gifts with which you are endowed..."* (WNT), *"And that special gift of ministry you were given...keep that dusted off and in use."* (MSG)

Was this his way of telling Timothy (and us), "Move it, or lose it!" Maybe he would've been more contemporary in his colloquialisms with us and challenged us with, "Bust a move!" I wouldn't be surprised, since I've said it to myself, and sometimes, sensed the Holy Spirit saying to me, *Bust a Move!* That word "move" is pretty interesting. Let me share with you what I discovered about it.

In John 15:5, the Lord said to His disciples (and us), *"Whoever lives in Me and I in him bears much (abundant) fruit."* (see John 15:5) In Volume 1 (Fair & Legal) of this book series, I alluded to our responsibility to not only have or bear fruit, but to also *be* fruit. While studying for a later chapter, I discovered something about the word bear, as it relates to us, as offerings or fruit. The Greek word for *"bear"* as it appears in John 15, is *phero* (fer-o). Some of the meanings of the word phero are *be, bring (forth)*, and *move."*

With this additional study and new discovery of definitions, I am led to believe that our Lord's desire is that we not only have fruit, but to bear or *be* and *bring forth* fruit! It's not a matter of this, or that. The fact of the matter is that it's *this <u>and</u> that*! And not only should we be the fruit – but we should also be *moved* to *"much (abundant) fruit."* When we do this, our *"...Father is honored and glorified..."* (see John 15:5, 8).

Everything We Need Is In The Seed!

Another such promise is *"<u>Everything we could ever need</u> for life and godliness has <u>already been deposited</u> in us by His <u>divine power...</u>"* (2 Peter 1:3 TPT emphasis added) Because we were preapproved and prepackaged with His promises, we don't have to pace the floor, pondering if He will keep His promises. We can confidently declare, like the Psalmist, *"I will cry to God Most High, Who performs on my behalf and rewards me [Who brings to pass His purposes for me and surely completes them]!" "The Lord will perfect that which concerns me;"* (Psalm 57:2; 138:8a respectively)

Similar to the Psalmist David, the Apostle Paul confidently declared, *"I am convinced and sure of this very thing, that He Who began a good work in you will continue until the day of Jesus Christ [right up to the time of His return], developing [that good work] and perfecting and bringing it to full completion in you."* (Philippians 1:6) It's okay to share the same level of confidence, and be just as convinced as they were. However, there's a *catch*, or as some would say, there are "some strings attached." As confident and convinced as we are, we must also consider that there are some *terms and conditions* that must be met. I'll cover some of them in the following paragraphs.

"As a result of this, he has given you magnificent <u>promises that are beyond all price</u>, so that through the power of these tremendous promises you can <u>experience partnership</u> with the divine nature..." (2 Peter 1:4 TPT emphasis added) OK, let's talk about some *terms and conditions*: Although God has provided us with precious promises, and even though they're *packed with power*; they will not make the *intended impact* on our lives or in the lives

It's All We Can Eat!

of others, without an important ingredient: *partnership*! It is imperative that we understand that God's promises will be unproductive and even impotent in our lives, *if we don't partner with Him*, in what He promises!

The appropriate response to receiving our *precious* or *"magnificent promises"* from The Almighty, is *reciprocation*. Our reciprocation is rendered through our *participation* – more specifically, *our partnership*. The last part of the AMPC version of the above verse reads, *"...and become sharers (partakers) of the divine nature."* The Greek word used for *"partakers"* is *koinonos* (koy-no-nos). It means "a participant who *mutually* belongs and shares fellowship; a joint-participant." God has *shared* or implanted in us, His *"divine nature"* or DNA. Through His impartation, we were created *"in His image and likeness"* (see Genesis 1:26-28)

This placement or implanting of *"His image and likeness"* implies that we already have what we need to partner, be fruitful, multiply, and experience His magnificent promises. It is also an indication that our participation in the production of fruit, is *not* optional. It's not an option, because it is *essential* to us escaping *corruption*! After the opening clause about *"His precious and exceedingly great promises"* 2 Peter 1:4 continues, *"so that through them, you may escape [by flight] from the moral decay (rottenness and corruption) that is in the world..."* The Passion Translation reads, *"the corrupt desires that are of the world."*

I would consider a *corrupt desire* to be rejecting or refusing to cooperate or participate through partnership, the precious promises of God. He deposited in us his DNA – His divine nature in order to *"experience partnership"* – love and live fruitful lives as *"partakers."* His desire is for our development and distribution - not corruption, death, and decomposition! We must understand and instill in others, that it is imperative that we be *active participants* in our *escape* and rescue!

Don't Deny The Power Of Love!

As I pointed out previously, we possess precious promises. We also possess immense power. However, if we reject or refuse to remain connected to or in partnership with the Source and Provider of love and power, we will be consumed by *"the corrupt desires that are of the world."* As a result of our refusal to be loved and empowered to love, we will rebel, become corrupt, wilt, wither, and perish!

The Apostle Paul warned his young protégé Timothy, about such people when he wrote to him (and to us), *"For [although] they hold a form of piety (true religion), they <u>deny and reject and are strangers to the power</u> of it...Avoid [all] such people [turn away from them]."* (2 Timothy 3:5 emphasis added) The KJV reads, *"Having a form of godliness, but denying the power thereof..."* This *"form of godliness"* is actually *deformed*! It looks nothing like the power and love God has both, provided and prescribed for us to live by.

Let's peer again, into one of His precious promises and properties of the power He prescribed and provided for us: *"For His divine power has bestowed upon us all things that [are requisite and suited] to life and godliness, through the [full, personal] knowledge of Him Who called us by and to His own glory and excellence (virtue)."* (2 Peter 1:3) His *"goodness"* which is a fruit of the Spirit (see Galatians 5:22), and glory are so *potent*, that they have the *power to call, attract, or command* us to them and Him! The Greek word used for *"call"* is kaleo (kal-eh-o). It means to "call forth, invite, name" and "summon." Because this fruit of the Spirit *"goodness"* is part of our divine nature, we are also empowered to attract, invite, or summon with specificity, others to His glory, power, and life of godliness.

The Passion Translation reads, *"For all this was lavished upon us through the rich experience of knowing Him Who has called us by name and invited us to come to Him through a glorious manifestation of his goodness."* (2 Peter 1:3b emphasis added) See? I *told* you! We have personalized invitation to invoke His divine power, and release from within us, *everything we need* to live a godly and victorious lives. Yes, if we're *"willing and obedient, you will eat the good things of the land"* (see Isaiah 1:19) and experience *sweet victory*!

This *"life and godliness"* is our lifestyle – our ability to exemplify or personify the nature and love of God. Everything required to demonstrate, reflect, or display God's *"divine nature"* – His Love, was *deposited in us before our birth date*, by God! We are encouraged, *"Every spiritual blessing in the heavenly realm has already been lavished upon us as a love gift from our wonderful heavenly father, the father of our Lord Jesus Christ..."* (Ephesians 1:3 TPT emphasis added) Included in the *"love gift"* that was *"lavished upon us"* is God's grace, which was given *"in proportion to the measure of Christ's [rich and bounteous] gift."* (see Ephesians 4:7)

Knowing Is Not Enough!

Besides the properties of glory and goodness, another property of this *divine power* is *"the [full, personal] knowledge"* or *"rich experience of knowing Him Who has called us by name..."* This experience of knowledge is intrinsic to His *"precious promise"* for us to *"experience partnership with the divine nature."* As amazing and precious as these properties are, we must not become presumptuous in *erroneously assuming* that they are preprogrammed or automated! In addition to not being preprogrammed or automated, they are also unable to be mastered by a novice – they require *knowledge – knowledge on another level*!

As I stated at the beginning of this chapter, in the same way that faith by itself, is insufficient; knowledge in and of itself, is insufficient, as well. Knowledge or intelligence is insufficient to ignite and empower us to pursue or walk in purpose and prosper. Knowing is not enough, just like *believing* in God is *not enough*! Jesus said, *"So do the demons…"* (see James 2:19) It is *understanding what to do with* that knowledge, or *wisdom – how to appropriately apply the knowledge* in a way that as *effective or expedient* for us, and beneficial to others, that produces *power*!

The Greek word used for *"knowledge"* is *epignosis* (ep-ig-no-sis). It means "recognition of a particular point (directed towards a particular object); perception, discernment, intuition." It's from the verb *epiginosko* (ep-ig-in-oce-ko), which means "to know exactly, to recognize, to know through personal relationship, *experiential knowing, through direct relationship.*" An example would be "I come to know by directing my attention to him or it – I found out."

In the same way that *"knowledge"* of God is not *automated*, the divine nature or life of godliness is neither *automatic*, nor *optional*! We have to put the *work in*, if we're going to get the *fruit out*, and let our light shine, so that others see our good works – the *godliness*, and glorify God (see Matthew 5:16)! Everything we need to accomplish this is encapsulated in a seed. Enclosed in the seed are the precious promises, knowledge, and power. However there's another key component that causes the seed to grow: *cooperation*! More specifically, *our cooperation*. Our cooperation leads to *liberation* – the liberation or *release* of that which is *encased* in the seed!

It's All We Can Eat!

Synonymous with cooperation, is participation, and as it pertains to this chapter, I'll add *partnership*. Our partnership – our *participation* or cooperation not only leads to liberation, but it also leads to *activation* and *elevation*! It's like the muscles we were given at birth. If we want them to be bigger, stronger, or toner (defined); we have to add to them, by *exercising* them! We can't just lay hands on them, and pray to God for transformation. He did His part, by *providing* us with them. It's now up to us to *partner* with Him, by providing our *participation*.

In the same way that the seeds for our muscle development and definition, are available, inside of us, awaiting the activation of them; so do the promises, faith, and purposes await our activation. Our participation prompts activation, and the activation eventually leads to *elevation* or *graduation*. We were not preordained to live impotent, purposeless, incompetent lives. That's because impotence inspires incompetence.

Instead, we were prepackaged with the most potent Power Source presented to mankind! No matter what stage or state in life we find our lives or bodies in – even if we feel emotionally, mentally, mortally, or spiritually *dead*; there's room and we have the right to restoration! We've been supplied with – our lives are *infused* with the Spirit of God! We are commanded, *"Be sober naturally infused with strength through your life-union with the Lord Jesus."* (see Ephesians 6:10 TPT)

Whenever doubt reaches out to rob us of our faith, we must remind ourselves, *"I have <u>strength for all things</u> in Christ Who empowers me [I am ready for anything and equal to anything through Him <u>Who infuses inner strength into me</u>; I am self-sufficient in Christ's sufficiency]."* (Philippians 4:13 emphasis added) We are also encouraged, *"And if the Spirit of Him Who raised up Jesus from the dead* *dwells in you, [then] He Who raised up Christ Jesus from the dead will also restore to life your mortal (short lived, perishable) bodies through His Spirit Who dwells in you."* (Romans 8:11) Therefore, we have *everything that we need* to activate, cultivate, and participate in the life a purpose that God predestined for us.

Our *precious promises* and *measure of faith* are much alike, in the sense that they are like our *muscles*. Along with the similarity of being supplied to us by God, in order to experience their maximum benefits, they must be *added to* and *exercised*! Everything embedded in our muscles and in our souls and spirits must be *added to*, or actually *released* by exercising – *working* what we've *already* been given! In order for things to grow and produce – in order for us to be *fruitful*, we must work or cultivate what has been implanted or imparted to us. Otherwise, they will lie dormant, and undeveloped within us, while we remain weak, powerless, and fruitless. In other words, because of our lack of activation, cultivation, and participation, we will experience spiritual *constipation*!

This concept of activating and subsequently, adding to and cultivating, is a lot like lifting weights properly. Some secondary muscles will subsequently grow and develop, as a consequence of us exercising or cultivating the primary muscles. Again, it's *not automatic*. The term used in Hebrews 5:14 is *"...by reason of use..."* (KJV) Other translations read, *"trained by practice"* (AMPC), *"trained by constant practice"* (ESV), *"through training"* (NLT), and *"through repeated practice"* (AFV). Therefore, we have no excuse for not *exercising* or *adding* to our promises. It is in engaging in adding to our promises, other elements – starting with faith, that activation, growth, and acceleration occur. However, again, it's not automatic. We must activate or initiate each step in the process. It requires our persistence and what is described as *"diligence."*

It's All We Can Eat!

It's "All We Can Eat!", Family. Let's Make Things Happen!

PART 2
Love Must Be Developed & Distributed

Chapter 8
Love Demands Diligence!

"For this very reason, adding your diligence [to the divine promises], employ every effort in exercising your faith to develop virtue (excellence, resolution, Christian energy), and in [exercising] virtue [develop] knowledge (intelligence)"
(2 Peter 1:5)

Please, Have Some More!

Sometimes, if we don't remember the *"reason"* or the *why* for what we're doing, or for *Whom*, we're doing them, we may relax or reduce our work, or even worse; relinquish or abandon our responsibilities, and retreat to a life of randomness, irresponsibility, restlessness, irrelevance and potential *ruin*!

So, to reduce the risk of us failing to remember our *why*, or recognize for *Whom*, we're doing what we do, let me refresh our memory: *"By his divine power <u>God has given us everything we need</u> for living a godly life. We have received all of this <u>by coming to know him</u>, the one who called us to himself <u>by means of his marvelous glory and excellence</u>. And because of his glory and excellence, <u>he has given us great and precious promises</u>. These are the promises <u>that enable you to share his divine nature</u> and escape the world's corruption caused by human desires."* (2 Peter 1:3-4 NLT emphasis added)

The Greek word for *"escape"* is *apopheugo* (ap-of-yoo-go). Besides meaning "to flee from", it is recognizing the *need to move on*. It conveys the sense of *separation* in that it is "a *full breaking away* from the previous situation." This reminds me of how our God command us, *"Do not be conformed to this world (this age), [fashioned after and adapted to its external, superficial customs], but be transformed (changed) by and be [entire] renewal of your mind [by its new ideals and its new attitude] ..."*

By *"coming to know Him"* when He calls us by His *"glory and excellence"* and remaining connected to Him, our minds are renewed, and we're reminded of His *"precious promises"*, as well as what He has already prepared us to do. Because God has deposited His *"divine power"* in us already, we have the ability – *everything we need* to do this – to escape the corruption, not be conformed to this world, and share His *"divine nature"* with others. When we do this, we prove *"what is the good and acceptable and perfect will of God, even the thing which is good and acceptable and perfect [in His sight for you]."* (see Romans 12:2) It's been said that "Sharing is caring." I'd like to add to that, *Loving is sharing, and sharing is caring*! We don't do it for the "Gram" (Instagram). We do it for the *Glory* of God!

It Has To Add Up!

Now that we have refreshed our memory with the reason why, let's look at the appropriate response. But before we do, let's revisit Romans 12, where Paul wrote, *"Beloved friends, what should be our proper response to God's marvelous mercies?"* (see Romans 12:1 TPT) Other translations read, *"And so, dear others and sisters, I plead with you…"* (NLT), *"Therefore, I exhort you…"* (BLB), *"I beseech you therefore…"* (KJV), *"…on account of God's mercies…"* (BSB), *"in view of all we have just shared about God's compassion, I encourage you…"* (GWT)

As you observed from the opening lines of various translations, there is something we are to address with a sense of urgency. We must address it, by *adding* to it! The *something*, or the *it* is our *diligence*. When the Apostle Peter inserted that word in the instructions to the Church (add to us), the implication was that *we already had it*, just like we already had the *precious promises*, our *faith*, and His *power*. Let's study the sense of urgency from alternate versions.

Peter's perspective and instruction from parallel translations read, *"Do your best to improve your faith by adding…"* (CEV), *"try your hardest to furnish your faith…"* (CJB), *"having applied all diligence besides…"* (AFV), *"adding, on your part, all earnestness…"* (WNT) *"make every effort to supplement your faith…"* (ESV), *"you must do your utmost from your side…"* (Phillips), *"make every effort to respond to God's promises…"* (NLT), *"And you, employing all care, minister in your faith…"* (DRA), *"So don't lose a minute in building on what you've been given…"* (MSG), *"do your best [make every effort; strive] to add these things to [or increase these things in] your lives…"* (EXB), *"So devote yourselves to lavishly supplementing your faith…"* (TPT) (2 Peter 1:5 emphasis added) The Aramaic can be translated *"by being under the weight of all these gifts."*

So, basically, the *reason* is because God *already* did His part, by making the deposit. He preordained, equipped, empowered, and promised us. In other words, He has *already* provided – He has given us a gift basket filled with all of the fruit (or at least the seed) we will ever need! Our *response* should be *to do our part*, by taking what was deposited, and *applying* with all diligence, everything necessary to *furnish* our faith. The software has already been preloaded or preinstalled. It is perfect and complete. However, our faith *isn't* perfected or completed. Therefore, we must *respond* to God's precious promises by *improving* on our faith, by *building* on what we've been given. We must see mixing, *supplementing*, or adding to our faith, as *ministry*. It is imperative that we don't procrastinate, but instead, *devote* ourselves to *increasing* or *"lavishly supplementing"* our faith. In other words, we have to *give it our all*, because as the 70s Funk Band *Heatwave* sang, *Ain't No Half Steppin'*!

Since half-steppin' is insufficient, let's see how and why we should give ourselves wholly or *diligently* to adding to our faith. In other words, why and how we must *feed* our faith. The Greek word used for *"adding"* is *epichoreogeo* (ep-ee-khor-ayg-eh-o). It means "to furnish besides, i.e. fully supply, aid, or contribute – minister (nourishment, unto)." My Bible footnotes define *epichoreogeo* as "to fully support the chorus or to completely choreograph."

I get the idea that *doing our part and adding to our faith* is similar to adding our portion or *voice to the song*, and supplying our part – *our steps or moves to the choreography* or *dance routine*. What I also found interesting, concerning steps, is that my Bible describes the section of 2 Peter 1:5-11 as *Faith's Ladder of Virtue*. To me, this means that in the same way that it takes more than one rung or step for a ladder to be considered a ladder that elevates us; it takes more than one characteristic or virtue being added to our faith for it to constitute being a *ladder of faith*!

The Greek word used for *"applying"*, which is somewhat synonymous with *"adding"*, is *pareisphero* (par-ice-fer-o). It means "to bring in, bear in alongside, i.e., introduce simultaneously." It is also defined as "bring deeply into, i.e., from very closely beside – "personally carry through." It refers to carrying through with real personal involvement (energy), and emphasizes the need of the Believer's deep, personal involvement in the faith life. As I was proofreading this, I was reminded of how the Precious Blood of Jesus was *applied* to us – bringing us *deeply* into the family of our Heavenly Father, and the Holy Spirit has come *very closely beside* – in fact, He lives inside of us!

Merely adding is inadequate. Simply supplying is insufficient. We must be *intimately involved, emphatically or enthusiastically engaged* in our efforts to do so. It is so crucial to our calling, that we "lavishly supply" or "diligently add" to our faith. We must dedicate ourselves to *everyday diligence*!

The Hands Of The Diligent

The Greek word used for *"diligence"* is *spoude* (spoo-day). It means "speed, haste, earnestness, enthusiasm." It is demonstrating *earnest care*. More specifically, for the Believer, it means *"quickly obeying* what the Lord reveals is *His priority*. It's like choosing the *God ideas* over the good ideas, the *best* over the better, the *more important* over the important, *purpose* over preference, etc. Besides meaning "constant and earnest effort to accomplish what is undertaken", there's also another word related to *diligence* – the Latin word *diligere*, which means to "single out, value highly, prize" and "love." So, when we are adding our *"diligence [to the divine promises]"*, we are demonstrating that we value highly or *love God* and *prize* His promises!

God has given us great clarity, concerning diligence. It is written, *"He becomes poor who works with a slack and idle hand, but the hand of the diligent makes rich."* (Proverbs 10:4) *"The hand of the diligent will rule, but the slothful will be put to forced labor."* (Proverbs 12:24) *"Do you see a man diligent and skillful in his business? He will stand before kings; he will not stand before obscure men."* (Proverbs 22:29)

It's quite simple: the hard (diligent) workers control, govern, experience promotions, power and dominion, become wealthy, and will stand before dignitaries – persons of prominence, and even kings! Their *gift of diligence* and *skillfulness* will open doors – make room for them and *bring them into the presence of great people* (see Proverbs 18:16).

It's All We Can Eat!

God blesses the work done by the hands of the diligent, and will in fact, bless the hands that *do* the work! (see Deuteronomy 28:12) They live large, with a lifestyle of the rich and famous.

While on the other hand, the slackers or slothful – those who sit on their hands (and gifts), become unsuccessful, poor and suffer in poverty. In a sense, they become slaves to their poor decision to *not* be diligent. They also end up as *servants* of those who decided to serve God with their diligence! They are only observers of success and the successful, while *enslaved* in obscurity!

While studying, I noticed in my footnotes for 2 Peter 1:5 from The Passion Translation, a variation which reads, *"by having added your intense effort."* This emphasizes that *we are expressly responsible* for exerting the energy (supplied by God) or making the effort to *supplement* or *diligently add* to our faith (also supplied by God)! This reminds me of hearing some preachers soliciting their congregations to encourage him to "Put your weight on it!" (when referring to a text or passage of Scripture).

The Aramaic can be translated *"by being under the weight of all these gifts."* I see it again, as *having everything we need* to do what God has commanded us to do. As I was taught years ago, "The power *to do* is in the *command.*" In other words, when God directs us to do something, implicit in the instructions is the *ability* to perform it – embedded in us, or deposited in the directions, is the *aptitude* to accomplish it!

We Must <u>Work</u> Our Faith!

Once we realize that we *already have everything we need* to do what God has commanded us to do, including the ability or aptitude; we must operate with the right attitude and *"employ every effort in exercising your faith…"* In other words, we must deploy our diligence to the faith that was already deposited in us. While *giving it everything we've got*, we must *work* or *exercise* our *"faith."* We must remember that we've been given by God, everything we need – *"that pertains to life and godliness"* – it's already been dispensed or deposited, but we need to *"develop"* it or *work it out* of us, and into the environment.

The Greek word for *"exercise"* is *gumnazo* (goom-nad-zo). Properly, it means "to practice naked or lightly clad i.e. train." Interesting, huh? Figuratively, it means "to train with one's full effort i.e. with complete physical, emotional force." It's exerting intensely – demonstrating the full concentration and discipline conducive to being in peak working condition. In other words, it's the type of workout or regimen that *requires constant rigorous* training. This is the type of exercise our Heavenly Father *expects* from us and our *faith*! If we're going to be proficient at fulfilling purpose and being fruitful – producing the harvests God has preordained and promised; we must put into practice, *this type of work*!

The Greek word for *"faith"* is *pistis* (pis-tis). Properly, it means "persuasion, assurance, belief, confidence, conviction, fidelity, trust, faithfulness." It can also mean "God's divine persuasion." Therefore, with the faith and faithfulness God has already deposited in us, we can proceed forward, fully persuaded – confident that we have the capacity and capability to carry out the assignments He has given us and be assured of His absolute faithfulness.

This caliber of conviction is required *"to develop virtue (excellence, resolution, Christian energy) ..."* Did you notice how that reads, *"develop"*, and not *add* or *create* virtue? That's because we already have a measure of virtue. However, it may be dormant, and require activation and development. What we're actually doing is affixing the virtue that we already have, to our faith. The Greek word for *"develop"* is *trepho* (tref-o). Properly, it means "enlarge, fully develop because of adequate nourishment." Figuratively, "to bring (experience) personal enlargement", i.e. spiritual development from being properly fed (nourished, taking care of). It also means "to make to grow, to nourish, provide for, feed."

When our faith is flourishing – enlarged and growing, due to adequate nourishment, our virtue – whether inactive or ineffective; can receive nourishment – be fed by our faith and become *revived* or *reinvigorated*! In other words, proper nourishment of our *preexisting* faith will provide the proper nutrients to our current portion of virtue, which will produce its *enlargement*!

This whole adding and supplying process has nuances that may not be easily noticeable. For example, the first *"add"* in 2 Peter 1:5 can actually be interpreted from the Greek word *pareisphero* (par-ice-fer-o), as apply or supply, and means "to bring in, bear in alongside, i.e. introduce simultaneously", and also "bring deeply into, i.e. from very closely beside." However, the instruction to *"add"* in the continuation of the command, is the Greek word *epichoreogeo* (ep-ee-khor-ayg-eh-o), which means (properly) "to *lavishly* supply, as it is suitable (apt) to outfit

It's All We Can Eat!

all that is needed to accomplish a *grand* objective; to richly supply or provide."

We see an example of *epichoreogeo* in the following verses: *"For because of Him the whole body (the church, in all its various parts), closely joined and firmly knit together by the joints and ligaments with which it is supplied, when each part [with power adapted to its need] is working properly [in all its functions], grows to full maturity, building itself up in love."* (Ephesians 4:16 emphasis added)

From Ephesians 4:16, we find that it's not only the body's *various parts'* need for its own, individual existence, nourishment, growth, and survival; but they recognize that part of their *"need"* is to *supply* or *nourish* *"each part"* with *power* in order that *they all* are nourished or fed, grow, and *enlarge*! In other words, because of the close connection – because they are *"closely joined"* to Jesus Christ, our Power Source, they have the power to *provide* or *supply power* to the other parts that are also *"closely joined"* and *all are built up* in the fruit of the Spirit, which is *Love*.

"...hold fast to the Head, from Whom the entire body, supplied and knit together by means of its joints and ligaments, grows with a growth that is from God." (see Colossians 2:19 emphasis added) Other translations read, *"But we receive directly from him, and his life supplies vitality into every part of his body through the joining ligaments connecting us all as one. He is the divine Head who guides his body and causes it to grow by the supernatural power of God." "...the source of life, Christ, who puts us together in one piece, whose very breath and blood flow through us. He is the Head and we are the body. We can grow up healthy in God only as he nourishes us." "...having nourishment ministered, and knit together,*

increaseth with the increase of God." (TPT, MSG, KJV respectively, emphasis added)

The implication of Colossians 2:19 is that our nourishment, growth, increase, enlargement, and empowerment *to provide power to other parts* is contingent upon us remaining connected to our Head – our Power Source, our Lord and Savior, Jesus Christ!

Valor & Virtue

As our faith or faithfulness is being nourished and enlarged, we develop our *"virtue"*, which was already attached or *"closely joined"* to our growing faith. Our desire and focus should be to obtain an *ever-increasing faith*, which will develop *ever-increasing* virtue. The Greek word for virtue is *arete* (ar-et-ay). It means (properly) "moral excellence which is displayed to enrich life." It also means "goodness, gracious act, uprightness."

This endowment of power *to be productive and fruitful* is intrinsic to our intimate relationship with Christ. This is why He said, *"I am the Vine; you are the branches. Whoever lives in Me and I in him bears much (abundant) fruit. However, apart from Me [cut off from vital union with Me] you can do nothing."* (John 15:5) The Passion Translation reads, *"...For as a branch severed from the vine will not bear fruit, so your life will be fruitless unless you live your life intimately joined to mine...As you live in union with me as your source, fruitfulness will stream from within you – but when you live separated from me you are powerless."* (see John 15:4-5)

I get the sense that this public *display to enrich life* is to enrich the lives of *others*, and not just goodness on display to impress others or to be ostentatious. Our virtue and valor is neither to draw attention to ourselves, nor add value to us, while devaluing others. Instead, it is intended to show others, *views of God's glory and versions of His love*. In other words, these *gracious acts* are not for self-gratification, but for *God's glorification*! This is why we are commanded to let our light shine, so that others see our *"moral excellence and your praiseworthy, noble, and good deeds and recognize and honor and praise and glorify your Father Who is in heaven."* (see Matthew 5:16)

It's through the *"exercising"* and developing of our virtue, that we *"[develop] knowledge (intelligence)"*, which we are invited to acquire. This invitation to invest in gaining intelligence – the gift of gaining *"the [full, personal] knowledge of Him"* is initiated or inspired by God Himself. More specifically, He *"called us by and to His own glory and excellence (virtue)."* (2 Peter 1:3) His virtue and glory are so great, and He values us so much, that His excellence invites us to know Him *more intimately*!

This is the desire that the Apostle Paul had, the desire that God has, and the desire that we should also have. He wrote, *"[For my determined purpose is] that I may <u>know Him</u> [that I may <u>progressively become more deeply and intimately acquainted with Him</u>, perceiving and recognizing and understanding the wonders of His Person <u>more strongly and more clearly</u>], and that I may in the same way <u>come to know the power</u> outflowing from His resurrection…as <u>to be continually transformed</u> [in spirit into His likeness even] …"* (Philippians 3:10)

In the same way that God's glory and virtue invites us to Himself, Wisdom also invites or invokes us into fellowship. However, we must be willing to answer, investigate, inquire, and acquire the intelligence (knowledge) and insight available to us. *"Listen! Wisdom is calling out. Reason is making herself heard."* At the summit of heights, on the highways, at the intersections, at the entrances of cities and towns, in doorways and hallways; Wisdom is *always* ready to speak to us!

Wisdom has counsel and sound knowledge, understanding, might and power; by which kings reign, rulers decree justice, princes rule, and nobles – even all the judges and governors of the earth are established. For whoever finds Wisdom finds life and draws forth and obtains favor from the Lord. This is part of the purpose for Him summoning us – it's so that He can *saturate* us with favor, *anoint* us with knowledge and *form us to flourish* (see Proverbs 8)!

"For the Lord gives skillful and godly wisdom; from His mouth come knowledge and understanding." (Proverbs 2:6) *"Wisdom is a gift from a generous God, and every word he speaks is full of revelation and becomes a fountain of understanding within you."* (TPT) Our Father delights in prospering us – in dispensing gifts of *wisdom* and *knowledge*. From His mouth, He releases Kingdom revelations. They are words to *live* by and *love* by – words of wisdom, by which we are to govern our lives and conversations. Our obedient devotion to abiding daily, in His Presence, is the key to unlocking the *treasures of true knowledge*, great skills, brilliant strategies, grace-filled thoughts, and understanding our design and destiny (see Proverbs 1). Therefore, when we are invited daily, we should enter His Presence *expeditiously*!

Since He calls us to Himself, *by His own glory and excellence (virtue)*, we know that He is willing to deposit it in us, when we get into His Presence. However, we must respond to what we receive in His Presence, by *meditating* on it, and *practicing* it! We are commanded, *"...if there is any virtue and excellence, if there is anything worthy of praise, <u>think on and weigh</u> and take account of these things [<u>fix your minds on them</u>]. <u>Practice what you have learned and received</u>, seen and heard and seen in me, and my role of your way of living on it, and the God of peace (of untroubled, and be stirred well be the one) will be with you."* (see Philippians 4:8-9 emphasis added) It's more pertinent and purposeful to *practice* what we receive, than it is to just possess it!

We can only think and meditate on what we know – the *knowledge* we have acquired. After we have pondered those things, we must then *exercise – put into practice*, what we have heard, learned, received, and seen in Him, in His Presence. In fact, Psalm 16:11 reads, *"You will show me the path of life; in Your presence is fulness of joy…" "…For you bring me a continual revelation of resurrection life, the path of the bliss that brings me face-to-face with you."* (TPT) Our Father wants us to *FaceTime* Him! When we seek His face, He shows us our future (see Psalm 139:5)! When we seek His face, we see and *"know the thoughts and the plans"* He has for us (see Jeremiah 29:11), and have *knowledge* of how to successfully walk the path or run the course He has *"set for us"* (see 1 Corinthians 9:24-25, Hebrews 12:1) Also, in doing so, others will *see* Him in *us* and perhaps, come into the *knowledge* of Him, for themselves!

The Greek word for *"knowledge"* or "knowing" is *gnosis* (gno-sis). It is a doctrine or wisdom gleaned from *personal experience* or a direct relationship. In the same way that we *"love Him, because He first loved us"* (see 1 John 4:19), we *know* Him, because He first *knew* us (see Isaiah

43:1, Jeremiah 1:5). In fact, David declared, *"Lord, you know everything there is to know about me."* (Psalm 139:1 TPT) He continued his discourse, *"Your eyes saw my unformed substance, and in Your book all the days [of my life] were written before ever they took shape, when as yet there was none of them."* (Psalm 139:16)

David could make such declarations, because he accepted His invitations, and invested times of intimacy in His Presence. Therefore, he possessed personal knowledge – he had *functional* (working), *first-hand experiences* with the Father. Due to his *direct relationship* with Him, he took delight in *knowing* Him and being *known* by Him! David *knew* and *acknowledged*, *"Wonderful are Your works, and that my inner self knows right well...How precious and weighty also are Your thoughts to me, O God! How vast is the sum of them!"* (see Psalm 139:14-17)

Another good example of knowledge due to *direct relationship* or *personal experiences*, would be the story of Samaritan woman – more specifically, the townspeople. Her initial invitation was, *"Come, see a Man Who has told me everything that I ever did!"* *"So the people left the town and set out to go to Him...Now numerous Samaritans from that town believed in, and trusted in Him because of what the woman declared and testified..."* Apparently, her enthusiasm and *knowledge* of Him was influential!

After staying with them a couple of days, due to their request, *"Then many more believed in and adhered to and relied on Him because of His personal message [what He Himself said]."* However, the key to this story for me, and as it pertains to my point, is what the people of the town told the woman *with direct, personal knowledge and experience*: *"And they told the woman, Now we no longer believe (trust,* *have faith) just because of what you said; <u>for we have heard Him ourselves [personally], and we know</u> that He truly is the Savior of the world, the Christ."* (see John 4:4-42)

She didn't just want to *know* and be known by The Lord (1 Corinthians 8:3), she wanted *others* to *know* Him, and be known by Him! Unless our knowledge is based on *personal experiences* and *direct relationships*, I really doubt if we can classify it as *knowledge*. At best, it's conjecture or speculation. Furthermore, because our credibility would be questionable, I'm not certain how many we could convince to "Come, see a Man – The Master & Messiah!" I am so grateful that God takes the guesswork out of knowing Him!

Food For Thought

"And [exercising] knowledge [develop] self-control, and in [exercising] self-control
[develop] steadfastness (patience, endurance), and in [exercising] steadfastness
[develop] godliness (piety),"
(2 Peter 1:6)

Our Redeemer is recorded as saying, *"My food (nourishment) is to do the will (pleasure) of Him Who sent Me and to accomplish and completely finish His work."* (John 4:34) We must never mistake, nor take the credit for *Who's actually doing the work* and Who the *"work"* belongs to! We may be the ones seen, and the work may also be seen; but it is unmistakably *"the will (pleasure) of Him"* and *"His work."* We are merely *"His workmanship"* (see Ephesians 2:10) When it comes to the working, cultivating, and carrying it out to completion; we are cautioned, *"[Not in your own strength] for it is <u>God Who is all the while</u>*

effectually at work in you [*energizing and creating in you the power and desire*], *both to will and to work for His good pleasure and satisfaction and delight."* (Philippians 2:13 emphasis added)

Although we may sometimes, become consumed with carrying out His will, we must not forget – we can't *get it twisted*: it is God, *through the fruit of the Spirit*, Who will *"...make you what you ought to be and equip you with everything good that you may carry out His will; [while He Himself] works in you and accomplishes that which is pleasing in His sight..."* (Hebrews 13:21 emphasis added) Some of us, as children, and maybe even as adults, may have wished we had Superpowers, when in fact, *we already do*! As I've reminded myself, I now remind you, *"...the Word of God, which is effectually at work in you who believe [exercising its superhuman power in those who adhere to and trust in and rely on it]."* (1 Thessalonians 2:13 emphasis added)

Once we are aware of our *Superpowers*, we can apply this *knowledge* – use the bits of impartation, information, and inspiration as a sort of *nutritional supplement* that we consume and meditate on, as we strengthen ourselves and proceed in our development process. Knowledge is necessary for us to effectively engage in and develop *"self-control"*, which is necessary in our navigating through life and living it in *godliness*.

Without adequate *self-control* (love) we won't *see* properly, and without acute eyesight or clear vision, we can cause damage or create dangerous conditions. And these conditions could culminate in disaster, or even destruction! *"Where there is no vision [no redemptive revelation of God], the people perish..."* (Proverbs 29:18) Other translations read, *"When there is no clear prophetic vision, people quickly wander astray..."* (TPT) *"If people can't see what God is doing, they stumble all over themselves..."* (MSG) *"When there is no vision [no revelation of God and His word], that people are unrestrained..."* (AMP)

A person without self-control (love) is undisciplined and can *easily* become a pernicious person – not only to others, but also to *themselves*, because they *voluntarily* make themselves *vulnerable*. They expose themselves to be attacked and exploited. In other words, a person who lacks (love) self-control is a self-destructive person. An uncontrolled, undisciplined or *self-control deficient* person is also an *unprotected* person! *"He who has no rule over his own spirit is like a city that is broken down and without walls."* (Proverbs 25:28)

If we *"cast off restraint"* and reject *"developing"* self-control, and would rather rebel and live our lives without it; we run the risk of living undisciplined, *defenseless* lives, which could result in our *ruin*! The Passion Translation of Proverbs 25:28 reads, *"If you live without restraint and are unable to control your temper, you're as helpless as a city with broken-down defenses, open to attack."*

That last verse inspired me to revisit Proverbs 29:18, and reveal some other versions which read, *"Where there is no revelation, people cast off restraint..."* (NIV), *"When people do not accept divine guidance, they run wild..."* (NLT), *"Where there is no word from God [vision; prophecy], people are uncontrolled..."* (EXB) *"Without guidance from God law and order disappear..."* (CEV) *"A nation without God's guidance is a nation without order..."* (GNT) *"Without a Vision is a people made naked."* (YLT) Wow, talk about being *exposed* and *vulnerable* or *naked and ashamed*! We see, from these supplemental translations, the severity of harm that we can subject ourselves to, if we choose to live without *self-control*. Such an undisciplined lifestyle leads to a disappearance of order or *disorder*!

Besides casting off restraint, a lack of self-control also causes us to remove boundaries, break barriers, and go beyond breaches. As a result, we may experience issues or calamity of catastrophic proportions! We are warned, *"...whoever breaks through a fence or a [stone] wall, a serpent will bite him. Whoever removes [landmark] stones...will be hurt with them, and he who fells trees will be endangered by them."* (see Ecclesiastes 10:8-9) There are some who may say, "Rules were made to be broken!" Depending on the rule, and the level of the lack of restraint; the repercussions could leave more than the rule broke – it may result in bones broken, or dreams and lives *shattered*!

Self-control is a sort of distraction deterrent, or irrelevance repellant. It helps us to stay disciplined and focused. Self-control assists in being selective in the placement of, or prioritizing people and projects. In other words, we are able to easily identify and designate what is more relevant or really important – giving them the appropriate position on our agenda or schedule. Self-control helps us to become "Highly Effective People." We not only know what to do, we also know what *not* to do! Therefore, we can politely, but firmly say, "No, thank you" when people invite, or even attempt to *entice* us away from pursuing our purpose.

Without self-control, we can't become the *highly effective* people God *preordained* and *expects* us to be. Instead, we will be inept – incapable of doing or unavailable to do what He has designed and designated us to be and do.

As I alluded to above, without self-control, our sight is impaired. In this state of mind, we will find ourselves following after and engaging in the wrong activities – the *antithesis* of our God ordained assignment! We won't do what we should do, and instead, we will do what we *shouldn't* do!

I believe that the Apostle Paul, at some point, suffered from a lack of self-control. Yes, the same one who commanded, *"...be strong in the Lord, and in the power of His might."* (Ephesians 6:10), and *"I can do all things through Christ who strengthens me."* (Philippians 4:13), also confessed, *"For I fail to practice the good deeds I desire to do, but the evil deeds that I do not desire to do are what I am [ever] doing."* (Romans 7:19 emphasis) So, as you can see, as smart and as strong as we are, or think we are; without *exercising and developing self-control*, we can find ourselves undisciplined, struggling with, and subsequently succumbing to the sometimes subtle, but strong stranglehold of the sin of disobedience!

The Greek word for self-control is *egkrateia* (eng-krat-i-ah). It means "mastery." More specifically, "self-mastery, self-restraint" and "continence, temperance." According to Thayer's Greek Lexicon, self-control is "the virtue of one who masters his desires and passions, especially his sensual appetites." Properly defined, it is "dominion within" i.e. proceeding out from *within* oneself, but *not by oneself*." For the Believer, this can only be accomplished – this virtue is vested in us by *"the fruit of the Spirit"*, Who lives in and flows through us, in proportion to *our union with Christ*. That's why we're reminded, *"For in Him, we live and move and exist [that is, in Him we actually have our being] ..."* In other words, *"It is through him that we live and function and have our identity..." "and he gives us the power to live, to move, and to be who we are."* (Acts 17:28 AMP, TPT, CEV respectively)

So, in essence, being self-controlled is actually being *Spirit-controlled*, and by being *Spirit-controlled*, we are able to excel and exercise *"dominion."* In Genesis 1:26, God gave us a glimpse of His glorious plan for us. What was included in His plans – what He was declaring as part of our destiny and how we were *designed*, is that we would have *"dominion"* over all of the wildlife. I believe that the *wildlife* included the wild life that lives *within us* when we're not *exercising and developing "self-control"* – when we're not allowing the fruit of the Spirit to manifest love or the expression of love listed as *"self-control"* in our lives.

They that live the *wild* life – those who lack *"self-control"* are *"those who are living the life of the flesh [catering to the appetites and impulses of their carnal nature] ..."* This lifestyle or mindset *"cannot please or satisfy God, or be acceptable to Him."* That's *"because the mind of the flesh [with its carnal thoughts and purposes] is hostile to God, for it does not submit itself to God's Law; indeed it cannot."* This is not the lifestyle that God has laid out for us. We are to be led by The Holy Spirit, not by our *"appetites and impulses."* When we're not engaging in self-control, we're not expressing love – to God, ourselves, or others.

This is why *"self-control"* (love) is so essential. As I stated earlier, it helps us to stay disciplined and focused. It assists us in being selective in the placement of our priorities, and we not only know what to do, we also know what *not* to do! Therefore, we will have the insight, energy, and incentive to say, "No" when we're invited, or even *enticed*

It's All We Can Eat!

to engage in activities antithetical to God's *calling* on our lives. When we're *self-controlled*, we're living our lives submitted, directed and controlled by the fruit of the Spirit, and we're equipped and empowered to *make things happen*! We're reminded, *"But you are not living the life of the flesh, you are living the life of the Spirit, if the [Holy] Spirit of God [really] dwells within you [directs and controls you] ..."* (see Romans 8:7-9)

It's "All We Can Eat!", Family. Let's Love Diligently!

Chapter 9
Strengthened To Be Steadfast!

"...and in [exercising] self-control [develop] steadfastness (patience, endurance),"

As stated above, self-control sets us up for *"steadfastness."* Like all of the other elements in the *development* process, *"steadfastness"* is *essential* – it's not optional, nor negotiable! In fact, we are commanded, *"Therefore, my beloved brethren, be firm (<u>steadfast),</u> <u>immovable</u>, always abounding in the work of the Lord [always being superior, excelling, doing more than enough in the service of the Lord], knowing and being continually aware that your labor in the Lord is not futile [it is never wasted or to no purpose]."* (1 Corinthians 15:58)

The Greek word for *"steadfast"* is *hedraios* (hed-rah-yos). Properly used, it means to "sit (solidly-based, well-seated). Figuratively, "firm – morally fixed; firm in purpose (mind); "well-stationed (securely *positioned*), not given to fluctuation our "moving off course." This definition reminds me of Colossians 1:23, which reads, *"[And this He will do] provided that you continue to stay with and in the faith [in Christ], <u>well-grounded and settled and steadfast, not shifting</u> <u>or moving away from the hope</u> [which rests on and is inspired by] the glad tidings (the Gospel) ..."* (emphasis added) We must not allow ourselves to be moved by our emotions or through our senses. Instead, we must remain *"steadfast"* and *inspired* by the Holy Spirit and His reminders of the Gospel.

The simple strategy to being strengthened is being *still*. The Lord will not command us to do anything that He isn't willing to do. It's written, *"And therefore the Lord <u>[earnestly] waits [expecting, looking, and longing] to be</u> <u>gracious to you</u>; and therefore He lifts Himself up, that He may have mercy on you and show loving-kindness to you. For the Lord God is a God of justice."* Because He wants to grant us grace, He doesn't make it difficult for us to detect

It's All We Can Eat!

or discern or determine where He is. In fact, He is *so committed* to showing us compassion, *"He lifts Himself up"* – He *rises to reveal* Himself to us!

Because He is a *"God of justice*, He rewards His *just* or righteous ones. The reward for waiting on Him; especially when times are rough and we would rather run, is an abundance of *blessings*! *"Blessed (happy, fortunate, to be envied) are those who [earnestly] wait for Him, who expect and hope and long for Him [for His victory, His favor, His love, His peace, His joy, and His matchless, unbroken companionship]!"* (Isaiah 30:18 emphasis added) This looks a lot, like *the fruit of the Spirit*, to me!

Those rough times, when we don't recognize His Presence and protection, are when we must remain resilient and respond by saying, *"And I will wait for the Lord, Who is hiding His face from the house of Jacob; and I will look for and hope in Him." "While I wait for God as long as he remains in hiding, while I wait and hope for him."* (Isaiah 8:17 AMPC, MSG respectively, emphasis added) We must be willing to *wait as long as it takes*. It's *never* correct to put God on a clock or calendar! No matter how long the trial or trouble – even when we can't track or trace Him, we must trust and hope in Him; knowing that He will cause us to triumph, and give us *"grace to help in good time for every need [appropriate help and well-timed help, coming just when we need it]."* (see Hebrew 4:16) His grace is amazing, and His timing is *always perfect*!

Whether we receive and experience abundance, or adversity; it's never for our benefit or punishment *only*. Our blessings should benefit others and our adversities should become teachers and tools that are advantageous to us and others, as well! Our blessings and adversities are *assigned* to be *signs* and *symbols* or *wonders*! *"Behold, I and the children and the Lord has given me are <u>signs and wonders</u> [that are to take place] ..."* (Isaiah 8:18 emphasis added)

Whether they're our natural, spiritual, or they're the *purposes* and *projects* God placed within us; we must see them as our *"children"* that He wants to use as *signs* of hope and *wonders* of His glory – first to us, and then to others! The Hebrew word used for *"sign"* can mean "banner" or "witness", and the one for *"wonder"* can mean "marvel, symbol" or "miracle." Whether He chooses abundant blessings, or unannounced adversity; God wants to work wonders and miracles in and through us, so that others can marvel and be motivated to *hope* in Him!

God reveals the riches of His Glory in and through us. When they see us, whether it's in seasons of abundance, or adversity; they should see Christ *in* us. We've got to be committed to seeing and letting them see Christ in us, *during* a crisis! If others are going to recognize and receive the riches, we must remind ourselves of this while we're waiting on Him, because it is *Christ in us*, Who is *"the Hope of [realizing the] glory."* (see Colossians 1:27)

Molded To Be Mountains

When I think of being *"steadfast"* or *"immovable"*, what comes to mind, are mountains and how they represent or symbolize *stability*. Mountains are massive and *unshakable*. In the same way that mountains have been formed by our Father (see Amos 4:13) and are fixed or immovable; He expects us to be formed, and *developed* or fashioned in our steadfastness, to the point that *we* are fixed, immovable, *fearless*, and *unshakable*! This is why the sons of Korah sang, *"Therefore we will not fear, though the earth should change and though the mountains be shaken into the midst of the seas,"* (Psalm 46:2) There should be *no one or nothing* that shakes us or moves us out of the will of God.

We must remember that steadfastness, or more specifically, *patience,* is *"the fruit of the Spirit"* or an *expression* of God's Love. His love and compassion comforts and *stabilizes* us. This love that He has for us is the same quality of love that we are to love Him back with, as well as love others with. Not that we can stabilize Him with it, but that in expressing love to Him, we are reminded and comforted that we are *established* in His love. We are assured, *"For though the mountains should depart and the hills be shaken and removed, yet My love and kindness shall not depart from you, nor shall My covenant of peace and completeness be removed, says the Lord, Who has compassion on you."* (Isaiah 54:10)

Mountains were not made or meant to move. They were formed by God to stand firm and symbolize God's strong, unshakable, stable, inseparable love for us, and His *everlasting* love and Word within us! He said, *"Sky and earth will pass away, but My words will not pass away."* (Matthew 24:35) No matter if immovable mountains were moved from the earth, or stars were removed from the sky, His *"steadfast"* love will *remain forever*! Therefore, *"Give thanks to the Lord, for he is good, for his steadfast love endures forever."* (Psalm 136:1 ESV)

The *permanence* of His love and Word in our lives is the same posture and position we should take, while in the process of developing *"steadfastness"* in our lives. In the same way that we are *"...persuaded beyond doubt...that neither death nor life, nor angels nor principalities, nor things impending and threatening nor things to come, nor powers, nor height nor depth, nor anything else in all creation will be able to separate us from the love of God which is in Christ Jesus our Lord"* (Romans 8:38-39); nothing, nor no one should slow down, stop, or separate us from developing a *"steadfast"* heart!

A Condition Of The Heart

I believe that *"steadfastness"* is a heart condition. The Greek word for *"steadfastness"* is *hupomone* (hoop-om-on-ay). It's "a patient enduring; a waiting behind." Properly used, it means "remaining under, endurance, perseverance; especially as God enables the believer to "remain (endure) under" the challenges He allots in life." So, to me, it's persevering under pressure – unshakable, while enduring uncomfortable conditions, because of being empowered and enabled by God. In other words, being strengthened, while submitted to God, and secure in what He has said.

I also believe that the state or status of our heart condition is contingent upon how we care for it. In order to get maximum efficiency from it, we must *"employ every effort in exercising your faith to develop…"* (2 Peter 1:5) In the natural, if we have a heart issue, we may visit our primary care physician, and get a referral to be examined by a cardiologist. Some of the recommendations that they may give us, are to change our diet, and get *exercise*.

In the spirit, we have *Someone*, often referred to as *The Great Physician*, a *Healthcare Provider*, Who provides us with *greater care than any cardiologist*! *"Then they cried to the Lord in their trouble, and he delivered them from their distress. He sent out his word and healed them, and delivered them from their destruction. Let them thank the*

Lord for his <u>steadfast love</u>, for his wondrous works to the children of man!"* (Psalm 107:19-21 ESV emphasis added) The NIV reads, *"... He rescued them from the grave. Let them give thanks to the Lord for his unfailing love..."* We are loved, nourished, healed, rescued, delivered, and provided for, with a *"steadfast"* and *"unfailing"* love. Therefore, we must love ourselves and others with this same quality of love or *fruit of the Spirit*.

Another *great* thing about our Physician, is that He *already* knows our heart condition. He just wants us to conclude and confess to Him, that we have a condition that only He can care for and correct. It's a *preexisting* condition. However, we don't have to worry about the cost or coverage, because it's already provided for in our healthcare plan that was purchased for us, before we were born. Essentially, *"...with the stripes [that wounded] Him we are healed and made whole."* (Isaiah 53:5)! We just have to set up our appointment, by stating, *"Create in me a clean heart, O God, and renew a right, persevering, and steadfast spirit within me."* (Psalm 51:10) The beauty is that the creation was done *beforehand*. The reality is that the state of our hearts – the *"steadfastness"* of them may just have to be *renewed* or *reactivated*!

Once the renewal or reactivation process has taken place, we can confidently declare like David, *"My heart is fixed, O God, my heart is steadfast and confident! I will sing and make melody."* (Psalm 57:7) The EXB version reads, *"My heart is steady [steadfast; ready], God; my heart is steady [steadfast; ready]. I will sing and praise [play a Psalm for] you."* To put this in the proper context, when this was composed – these were *not* words and thoughts he considered from the *comfort* of his palace. No, these are the

It's All We Can Eat!

comments, considerations, contemplations, and *convictions* of someone in a cave! He had been fleeing – he was forced to be a former friend, who was being *fiercely pursued* by his king, and his army, who had been converted into a *foe*!

Yet, in the midst of being passionately pursued, his mindset was one of such *confidence*, that he was *steady and ready* to throw a concert for his Provider, Creator, and Protector; instead of a pity party for himself! This was surely, a personification of *"steadfastness"*! I wonder if the cave where he confessed his confidence was at the base or side of a mountain – a mountain that reminded him of the safety, security, and stability, as well as the *unfailing* love, and *unmovable* faithfulness of his God. I wonder if the acoustics in that cave called his attention to commit to *"...constantly echo God's intense love..."* (1 Peter 4:8)

As we can see from this brief study from the story of David, *"steadfastness"* isn't developed during times of comfort and convenience. On the contrary, *confidence*, *endurance*, and *courage* are developed during times of confusion, trouble, inconvenience, trauma, and conflict! This is why we are reminded, *"Moreover [let us also be full of joy now!] let us exult and triumph in our troubles and rejoice in our sufferings, knowing that pressure and affliction and hardship produce patient and unswerving endurance. And endurance (fortitude) develops maturity of character (approved faith and tried integrity). And character [of this sort] produces [the habit of] joyful and confident hope of eternal salvation."* (Romans 5:3-4 emphasis added)

What I noticed, when looking at the above verse again, was that *"now"* is the time to give *joyful* notice to ourselves and others, even if *"now"* is when we're engulfed in trials or experiencing troubles! Hebrews 11:1 begins with, *"Now faith is..."* – not "Faith is..." or "*Then* faith is..." That's because it's in our current conditions (trials) or *now circumstances* (troubles), that *"steadfastness"* is constructed. In other words, the problems, afflictions, and pressures of our current life will cultivate, *"develop"*, and *"produce"* patience, endurance, maturity, integrity, and *"confident hope"* in our present, for our future deliverance. However, we must remain joyful *during the present pressures*, instead of waiting until we're pulled out of them, or when they pass over us!

    I believe that a key or core component to being steadfast is having a *healthy hope* for – an *optimistic outlook* on our future. In other words, having a hope so healthy and so strong – so formidable, that our lives and future are *fastened* or *fixed* to it! We can confidently fix our hope on our future – we can attach our hope to our future, because The Almighty has *authored* it! He said, *"For I know the thoughts and plans that I have for you...thoughts and plans for welfare and peace and not for evil, to give you hope in your final outcome."* (Jeremiah 29:11) *"I know what I'm doing. I have it all planned out – plans to take care of you, not abandon you, plans to give you the future you hope for."* (MSG) *"I will bless you with a future filled with hope – a future of success, not of suffering."* (CEV)

    Therefore, In the same way that we must exercise our faith, we must also exercise our hope. And in addition to exercising our hope, we must also exercise our steadfastness! Exercising our *"steadfastness"* produces additional dimensions and levels of hope. Our *exercising* or labor is prompted by love (*fruit of the Spirit*), and our *"steadfastness"* is inspired by our hope in Christ, and the thoughts and plans of God.

I believe this is why the Apostle Paul penned, *"...your work energized by faith and service motivated by love and unwavering hope in [the return of] our Lord Jesus Christ (the Messiah)."* (1 Thessalonians 1:3) Other translations read, *"your work produced by faith, your labor prompted by love, and your endurance inspired by hope..." "your work of faith and labor of love and steadfastness of hope..." "how you put your faith into practice, how your love motivates you to serve others, and how unrelenting is your hope-filled patience in our Lord Jesus Christ."* (NIV, ESV, TPT respectively) All three components or qualities: *faith*, *hope*, and *love* work together, as we *exercise* them – *put them into practice*; to energize, motivate, inspire, develop and produce *steadfastness*.

Although the focus of the above verse is primarily on hope in the return of Christ, the principle applies to us *now*, because *He is at work in us now* and our faith in Christ inspires us to hope from *now*, until the end of time. *"For we have become partakers of Christ if we hold the beginning of our confidence steadfast to the end."* (Hebrews 3:14 NKJV) We see our future – our prospects, promises, and plans God has for us – plans to prosper us and not harm us, to give us hope and a future – from our *now*; where we've *steadfastly* attached or anchored our souls to it!

Therefore, every moment is a *"now"* moment – and not just a *"now"*, but a *right now* moment! His Presence alone, provides us with the grace and strength to grab, grip, or grasp and hold onto His promises throughout our process! We are encouraged, *"[Now] we have this [hope] as a sure and <u>steadfast anchor of the soul</u> [it cannot slip and it cannot*

It's All We Can Eat!

break down under whoever steps out upon it – a hope] and reaches farther and enters into [the very certainty of the Presence] within the veil, Where Jesus has entered in for us [in advance] ..." (Hebrews 6:19-20)

It is there, in the *Secret Place of His Presence*, that we are encouraged and empowered to encounter Him and *"hold fast the hope..."* Since we've received an invitation and access is reserved, we must respond appropriately: *"And now we have run into his heart to hide ourselves in his faithfulness. This is where we find his strength and comfort, for he empowers us to seize what has already been established ahead of time – an unshakable hope! We have this certain hope like a strong, unbreakable anchor holding our souls to God himself. Our anchor of hope is fastened to the mercy seat..."* (see Hebrews 6:18-20 TPT emphasis added) It is when we *"seize"* or *fasten by love* and *through exercise*, the *unfadable* mercy of an *undefeated* God, our hope becomes *unshakable* and *unbreakable*! In such engagement and encounters, we become *established*!

Our adversary satan, wants us unstable. That's because he knows that when we are stable we are a *threat* to him! Therefore, he tries to instill in us, a spirit of fear, or douse us with doubt. That's because he knows that if we are doubtful or double-minded – if he can usher us into a state of instability, we will be *"...unstable and unreliable and uncertain about everything [he thinks, feels, decides]."* (James 1:8) So, he tries to use tragedies, trials and traumas to entrap us, or keep us transfixed on them, instead of trusting in God.

However, steadfastness *establishes* or stabilizes us during times when trials and trouble attempt startle us, and when tragedy and trauma try to terrorize or strike fear in us.

It's All We Can Eat!

During those *unsettling* times and in the midst of our *suffering*, we must *constantly* remind ourselves, *"And after you have suffered a little while, the God of all grace [Who imparts all of blessings and favor],* <u>*Who has called you to His [own] eternal glory*</u> *in Christ Jesus, will Himself* <u>*complete and make you what you ought to be, establish and ground you securely, and strengthen, and settle you.*</u>*"* (1 Peter 5:10 emphasis added)

I have a confession to make: In the past, and sometimes presently, I complicate matters, by having the wrong *mindset*. Having the wrong perspective has been problematic in the past, and I'm sure it will be in the future, if it persists. My point is that God's *process* of completing us and making us what we *"ought to be"* – His idea of how to *"establish and ground you securely, and strengthen, and settle you"* includes practice, pressure, prodding, plucking, pricking, prompting, pruning, etc. None of these appear to pleasant. However, this process is *necessary* in order to produce *"a peaceable fruit of righteousness to those who have been* <u>*trained by it*</u> *[a harvest of fruit which consists in righteousness – and conformity to God's will in purpose, thought, and action, resulting in right living and* <u>*right standing*</u> *with God]."* (see Hebrews 12:11)

What's important is not what part of the process we're in, nor how long the process will last. What's important is *what* and *who* we will become when we've *endured* the process! We're told that our suffering is only for *"a little while"* and we're also told that it is a tool for us to be *"trained by."* The process or *trial* is temporary, but the glory we receive is *eternal*! In fact, the Apostle Paul pointed out, *"[But what of that?] For I considered that the sufferings of this present time (this present life) are not worth being compared with the glory that is about to be revealed to us and in us and for us and conferred on us!"* (Romans 8:18)

"For our light, momentary affliction (this slight distress of the passing hour) is ever more and more <u>abundantly preparing and producing and achieving for us</u> an everlasting weight of glory [beyond all measure, excessively surpassing all comparisons and all calculations, a vast and transcendent glory and blessedness never to cease!]" (2 Corinthians 4:17 emphasis added) The experience we *endure* in our process is insignificant, in proportion to the *blessings, glory* and *duration* to enjoy what we receive, as a result of *remaining steadfast*! In other words, it's all working together for our good – it's *preparing, achieving,* and *producing* for us, who are *"steadfast" – "for those who love God and are called according to [His] design and purpose."* (Romans 8:28)

Therefore, we must remain steadfast, and not *"be weary well doing"* (we are doing well, because He is with us): *"for in due season we shall reap if we do not lose heart." "...we will reap a harvest of blessing if we don't give up."* (see Galatians 6:9 KJV, NKJV, NLT respectively) Therefore, we must be diligent. We can't be deceived, distracted, or have a divided heart about what we see. Instead, we must remain vigilant and focused – we must constantly *envision* what God is doing in us and what He has for us! *"For the vision is yet for an appointed time and it hastens to the end [fulfillment]; <u>it will not deceive or disappoint</u>. Though it tarry, <u>wait [earnestly] for it, because it will surely come</u>..."* (see Habakkuk 2:3 emphasis added)

We can consider this a guarantee, because He is *"the God of all grace [Who imparts all blessings and favor] ..."* (1 Peter 5:10) We can also consider it a guarantee because

He called us to His glory and by His glory, that we may receive glory. He declared, *"So shall My word be that goes forth out of My mouth: it shall not return to Me void [without producing any effect, useless], but it shall accomplish that which I please and purpose, and it shall prosper in the thing for which I sent it."* (Isaiah 55:11) He deposited His word in us, and deployed us into a process, and in our *steadfastness* – in becoming *established*, He eventually calls us to Himself, and we return to Him with a *harvest*!

This *harvest of righteousness* or right standing – being *established* is so precious and important to Him, that to ensure our success, He *"...will personally and powerfully restore you and <u>make you stronger than ever</u>. Yes, he will set you firmly in place and build you up. And he has all the power needed to do this – forever! Amen."* (1 Peter 5:10 TPT emphasis added) This goes back to what I alluded to earlier – He will make us what we *"ought to be and equip you with everything good... [while He Himself] works in you and accomplishes that which is pleasing in His sight..."* (see Hebrews 13:21) *"...may he work perfection into every part of you giving you all that you need to fulfill your destiny."* (TPT)

I can't ignore the fact that the term *righteousness* or *right standing* is used three times in *one* verse (Hebrews 12:11). That observation is an indication that God wants me to do an investigation and explanation. So, let's begin. The Greek word for *"righteousness"* is *dikaiosune* (dik-ah-yos-oo-nay). It means "justice, justness, righteousness." It is a justification or *divine* righteousness that God is the *Author* or *Source* of. It's the *divine verdict* or *approval* of God – what's *approved* or seen as *right* in the eyes of the Lord, upon *His examination*.

It's All We Can Eat!

Earlier in the day of this writing session, I learned another word related to or synonymous with righteousness. The words is *rightwiseness*, and as you might imagine, means righteousness. The word *rightwise* can mean "acceptable to God, conforming to divine law, virtuous, holy, of God, just in all dealings" and "incorruptible." In other words, it means *wise in that which is right* in the eyes of God. It's not something we can do, but what *only* God can determine.

As I did my word study on righteousness, in comparison to *steadfastness*, I considered the characteristics of who God called or counted as righteous – one who is *established*. It reminded me of a book I read, titled, *The Psalm 112 Promise*, by Apostle John Eckhardt. Within the pages of the book, a particular person is described.

It is said of them, *"<u>He will not be moved forever;</u> the [uncompromisingly] righteous (the upright, in right standing with God) shall be in everlasting remembrance. He shall not be afraid of evil tidings; <u>his heart is firmly fixed</u>, trusting (leaning on and being confident) in the Lord. <u>His heart is established and steady</u>, he will not be afraid while he waits to see his desire established upon his adversaries."* (Psalm 112:6-8 emphasis added) *"<u>Their circumstances will never shake them</u> and others will never forget their example. They will not live in fear or dread of what may come, <u>for their hearts are firm, ever secure in their faith</u>. Steady and strong, they will not be afraid, but will calmly face their every foe until they all go down in defeat."* (TPT emphasis added)

Here's what I saw, as I read these verses: First, they understand that whatever trial or pressure they're under, it's *only temporary*. Therefore, they are not shocked or shaken.

Instead, they remain *unmoved* and *unshakable*! Second, they take *ownership* and see their circumstances or experience*s* as *opportunities to be an example* to others! Because they are unbothered by the experiences, their *"example"* of being *established* and *remaining unmoved* will be *unforgettable* – remembered and retold *forever*!

Third, they don't submit themselves to *"a spirit of fear"* because they are *secure* and governed by a spirit *"...of power and of love and of calm and well-balanced mind and discipline and self-control."* (2 Timothy 1:7). Their heart is firmly fixed, steady and *established* in the Lord, the Source of their confidence. Therefore, they are not concerned about what they hear may come their way.

Fourth, they continually lean on and trust in, and have their confidence in the Lord with all their heart. They don't rely on their own insight or understanding. Instead, they acknowledge Him, in all their ways, and He gives them instructions and directions. They put all of their weight on Him, while they wait for their enemies to be defeated (see Proverbs 3:5-6).

Fifth, they understand that their confidence and competence to carry the weight or withstand the pressure of waiting is contingent upon *how* they wait on God. They know that the *appropriate* way is to *"Wait and hope for and expect the Lord; be brave and of good courage and <u>let your heart be stout and enduring</u>. Yes, wait for and a hope for and expect the Lord."* (Psalm 27:14 emphasis added)

They also realize that while waiting, those *"[who expect, look for, and hope in Him] shall change and renew their strength and power; they shall lift their wings and mount up [close to God] as eagles [mount up to the sun];*

they shall run and not be weary, they shall walk and not faint or become tired." (see Isaiah 40:31)

This is because they're not caught up in, and conformed to the current culture's customs. They're not stuck to society's superficial structure and standards. Instead, they live triumphantly, *even during trials*, because they are being *"transformed (changed) by the [entire] renewal"* of their minds. When we do this, we discover and discern *"...what is the good and acceptable and perfect will of God, even the thing which is good and acceptable and perfect [in His sight for you]."* (Romans 12:2) There's a *transformation* that accompanies *expectation*!

To the person who is confused, lacks confidence, is conformed to this world, and whose *heart* is not committed to the Lord; the trials and troubles that come may convince them that it's a curse. However, those whose *heart is stout*, have a *transformed mind*, and *expect and hope in Him*; see things *differently*! They realize that the eyes of the Lord *run* – they *roam* or *"...range throughout the earth to strengthen those whose hearts are fully committed to him."* (2 Chronicles 16:9 NIV)

They also realize that *"The eyes of the Lord are toward the [uncompromisingly] righteous and His ears are open to their cry."* (Psalm 34:15) 1 Peter 3:12a reads, *"For the eyes of the Lord are upon righteous (those who are upright and in right standing with God), and His ears are attentive to their prayer."* The Lord's eyes *"...rest upon the godly, and his heart responds to their prayers."* (TPT)

One reason why the Lord's eyes rest upon the righteous, is because He wants to *reveal* things to us. He said, *"I will instruct you and teach you in the way you should*

It's All We Can Eat!

go; I will counsel you [who are willing to learn] with my eye upon you." "... I will stay close to you, instructing and guiding you along the pathway for your life. I will advise you along the way and lead you forth with my eyes as your guide." (Psalm 32:8 AMP, TPT respectively) It doesn't matter if we are weak, weary, or worn out; if we're *willing to learn*, He will give us *wisdom* and *guide us*!

So, because of their confidence, and because they are *established* in, and sense the *security* of their *Salvation*; they never see themselves as cursed or feel like they're forsaken. Instead, they *believe*, and in fact, *know* that they are *blessed*! Their motivation and meditation is: *"[Most] blessed is the man who believes in, trusts in, and relies on the Lord, and whose hope and confidence the Lord is."* This man or woman is much like the trees spoken of in Scriptures, which are planted in the Presence or Court of the Lord (see Psalm 92:13), or *"...planted by the waters that spreads out its roots by the river; and it <u>shall not see and fear when heat comes</u>; but its leaf shall be green. It <u>shall not be anxious and full of care in the year of drought</u>, nor shall it cease yielding fruit."* (Jeremiah 17:7-8 emphasis added)

They are content *during* the circumstances, and their confidence continues to grow, because they've committed themselves to obey the command, *"<u>Do not fret or have any anxiety</u> about anything, but in every circumstance and in everything, by prayer and petition (definite requests), with thanksgiving, continue to make your wants known to God. <u>And God's peace [shall be yours</u>, that tranquil state of <u>a soul assured of its salvation</u> through Christ, and so fearing nothing from God and being content with its earthly lot of whatever sort that is, that peace] which transcends all understanding shall garrison and <u>mount guard over your</u>*

hearts and minds in Christ Jesus." (Philippians 4:6-7 emphasis added) Peace is poured or pumped into, and then permeates and pulsates throughout the *heart* of the steadfast – the *"soul assured of its salvation"*!

It's important to remind ourselves; especially during those seasons when our steadfastness is being developed, that we don't experience this type of peace, only when under perfect conditions. On the contrary, this peace can be cultivated *while in the center of chaos and when confusion is swirling* around us! When the winds of uncertainty are whirling, we should encourage ourselves with, "His grace is *sufficient* for me and His strength is *perfect* – it works best in my weakness! The Apostle Paul proclaimed, *"Therefore, I will all the more gladly Glory in my weaknesses and infirmities, that the strength and power of Christ (the Messiah) may rest (yes, may pitch a tent over and dwell) upon me!"* (see 2 Corinthians 12:9)

When our hearts and minds are set on *Who* and *Where* our strength and power rest, we remember and repeat to Him, *"You will keep in perfect and constant peace the one whose mind is steadfast [that is, committed and focused on You – in both inclination and character], Because he trusts and takes refuge in You [with hope and confident expectation]."* (Isaiah 26:3 AMP) It is always wise to recite back to Him, what we have read about Him, and heard Him say to us. It is a strategy that stirs us, strengthens us, and reinforces our faith, which *"comes by hearing"* (see Romans 10:17)

When we have a steadfast heart and mind, we also remember and repeat to Him, *"In peace [and with a tranquil heart] I will both lie down and sleep, For You alone, O Lord, make dwell in safety and confident trust."* (Psalm 4:8 AMP)

It's All We Can Eat!

This is because we have the assurance that He is our *Shelter* – He has showed up and has pitched at tent over, and become a *Shield* around us! We will not validate or verify that we are in the *"valley of the shadow of death"*, and will we not fear, nor will we *dread evil*, since *our Shepherd is with us*! (see Psalm 23)

I had an interesting dream on the night/slash morning before the writing of this paragraph. From what I remember, someone was reciting or reminding me of a familiar Bible verse. However, it wasn't verbatim, yet it has proven to be a very valuable lesson for me. This person, who I believe was the Holy Spirit, said to me, "With that same pressure, He will either *strengthen* you, so that you can *endure* it, or He will make a *way of escape* for you."

In my semi-conscious to state, I meditated on what He said, hoping to make it make sense. You see, I knew that it was a Biblical principle, but it didn't seem to be exactly what the Bible said. The more I meditated on it, the more awake I became. So, finally, at around 5:43 AM, still very sleepy, I picked up my phone and Googled, "Bible verse: but with the same amount of pressure, it will cause us to bear..." the result of my search was 1 Corinthians 10:13. I then, set an alarm with the scripture reference as the reason for the alarm, and went back to sleep.

That was really deep and super spiritual, right? (LOL) Hey, what can I say? I just told you that I was *sleepy* (LOL)! I just thank God that at least, I had the presence of mind to wake up and set an alarm about the dream, instead of just saying to myself, "I'll remember it in the morning.", and going back to sleep, and of course; *not remembering it* later!

It's All We Can Eat!

1 Corinthians 10:13, in part, reads, *"No temptation [regardless of its source] has overtaken or enticed you that is not common to human experience [<u>nor is any temptation unusual or beyond human resistance</u>]; but God is faithful [to His word – He is compassionate and trustworthy], and He will not let you be tempted beyond your ability [to resist], <u>but along with the temptation</u> He [has in the past and is now and] <u>will [always] provide the way out as well</u>, so that you will be able to <u>endure it</u> [without yielding, and will <u>overcome temptation with joy</u>]."* (AMP emphasis added)

What the Apostle was pointing out to the church at Corinth (and to us), is that in spite of that confusion, commotion or chaos, and no matter how unexpected, unimaginable, unpleasant, and *seemingly*, unyielding; it is *not* unbearable, uncommon, or unnecessary! In fact, the Apostle Peter penned, *"...For you know that your believing brothers and sisters around the world are experiencing the same kinds of troubles you endure."* (1 Peter 5:9 TPT) Unreasonable, and unhappy experiences are not *unique* to us, corporately, or individually – *we all* experience trouble and temptation. The Lord said that in this world – on Earth, we will experience *"many"* trials and tribulations (see John 16:33).

Instead of being taken down by the temptations, those with a steadfast heart, focus on the *compassion*, *faithfulness*, and *trustworthiness* of our Father. They know that *He knows* how much weight we can bear, and how long we can wait, *while bearing it*! He will not allow that weight, nor our *wait* to exceed our ability to bear it. Instead, He will introduce to us, and sometimes, escort us to our *exit strategy*. He will either take us out of it, before it takes us away from here, or *strengthen* us to withstand it – He refreshes and revitalizes us, to resist it, *while we wait* for rescue or restoration, and *as we rejoice*!

Unfortunately, too often, we prefer and pray for God to extricate us from the troublesome experiences, when He is well-aware that the *purpose* for the problem is to *expand our capacity* and *build endurance* in us, so that we are *better equipped* and *effective* for future service and projects. In His infinite wisdom, He realizes that taking us out of the entanglement, or extracting us from the entrapment would evacuate us away from the *very conditions conducive* to our growth and development. In fact, taking us out of the trouble, or away from the temptation too soon, actually *stunts* our growth!

I believe that this is why King David declared, *"The punishment you brought me through was the best thing that could have happened to me, for it taught me your ways."* (Psalm 119:71 TPT) *"My troubles turned out all for the best—they forced me to learn from your textbook."* (MSG) Instead of being distracted by the difficulties, traumatized by the trouble, or derailed by the drama; we should encourage ourselves with, *"...He will screen and filter the severity, nature, and timing of every test or trial you face so that you can bear it."* (1 Corinthians 10:13 TPT)

My interpretation of the dream – what I believe the Holy Spirit was saying to me is that there is no temptation that has overtaken me, except that which is common to man – including the temptation to quit or give up. There is no excuse, because everyone encounters the same temptations and has the same pressure applied to them to give up, quit, or give in to the pressure and temptations. In other words, *we're all under the same weight*. There is no pressure applied to us, that is not presented to others.

However, in the same way that our Father is *faithful* and *just*, to not let us be tempted beyond our *"ability and strength of resistance and power to endure...but will with the same temptation also make a way of escape..."* (KJV), He is *faithful during our periods of pressure*; to present us with a way to escape the excruciating experiences or empower us and provide us with the appropriate strength to endure them. His provision of either option will be *proportionate* to the pressure we're under! Therefore, no matter what we have to deal with, we must not get distracted or be in distress. There's no trauma, trial, or trouble that should be used to trap us, because God is with us and will use those same experiences of pressure, to *protect* us while we're under them, or *propel* us out of them!

Balanced In Confidence, Stabilized By Steadfastness

What helps us remain *steadfast* is remembering – constantly reminding ourselves, and *continuing* to have our *hope and confidence* in the Lord. As I alluded to above, *blessed* is the person that prizes – who realizes how *precious* – who recognizes how *rewarding* our *"hope and confidence"* is; *especially when we are under pressure!* We are cautioned, *"Do not, therefore, fling away your fearless confidence, for it carries a <u>great and glorious compensation of reward</u>. For you have need of <u>steadfast patience and endurance</u>, so that you may perform and fully accomplish the will of God, and thus <u>receive and carry away [and enjoy to the full] what is promised</u>."* (Hebrews 10:35-36 emphasis added)

If we cast off our *confidence*, we're left uncovered and unable to complete our assignment. If we *"fling away"* what *fortifies* us, we won't fulfil the mission. It's not just a nice thing to have – *"steadfastness"* is a *necessity*! It is *imperative* that we *possess* it! Otherwise, we can't perform and fully accomplish the objective – fulfilling the will of God, as well as receiving and enjoying our reward – what's presented to us: "*what is promised.*" To receive one, without the other, would be unbalanced and incomplete. The reward received – what's promised is our *soul's victory*. It is written, *"For you are reaping the harvest of your faith – the full salvation promised you – your souls' victory!"* (1 Peter 1:9 TPT)

Steadfastness stabilizes and balances us. In order to properly wait and *appropriately* develop, we need both balance and stability. They assist in us becoming *"stout-hearted."* We are commanded to *"let your heart be stout and enduring"* in Psalm 27:14. We are advised to *"be entwined as one with the Lord."* (TPT) I believe that sometimes, being *"entwined"* with the Lord is a work we must do, even when *we don't feel Him near us*! I'm not sure about you, but there have been many times in my life, when I didn't feel Him near, nor did I hear His voice. However, I had to *hope and expect* Him appear and speak to me, eventually! The verse continues, *"Yes, keep on waiting – for he will never disappoint you!"* (emphasis added)

David also had to *hope and expect* God on many occasions, *during difficult times*. Because he remained balanced and stabilized, he could confidently declare, *"In the day when I called, You answered me; and You strengthened me with strength (might and inflexibility to temptation) in my inner self."* (Psalm 138:3) Other translations read, *"you made me bold and stouthearted."* (NIV), *"you emboldened me and strengthened my soul."* (BSB), *"my strength of soul you increased."* (ESV), *"with your strength you strengthened me."* (GNT), *"thou shall multiply strength in my soul."* (DRB), *"You made my life large with strength."* (MSG), *"You responded and infused my soul with strength."* (Voice), *"You strengthened me deep within my soul and breathed fresh courage into me."* (TPT) The only way that we get to this stage and level of strength in our lives – the way we get to *live large*, is through hoping and expecting, while *waiting*!

In order to avoid someone reading this, to not get discouraged, I believe it is my duty to insert a disclaimer here: the Hebrew word for *"day"* in the passage above, is *yowm* (yome). Although it can mean a 24-hour period, such as *from one sunset to the next*, or a day such as from *sunrise to sunset*; it can also mean a "period of time" or a "season." What I found to be interesting; especially as it pertains to this topic, is that this word can also mean "to be hot; a day (as in the warm hours)." In other words, David could have been saying, "When it got *hot* – during a *time* when *the heat* was on – when things got *heated* in my life, I called out to You, and in that *season*, You strengthened me, so that I could remain *steadfast* that day!"

We cannot afford to be deceived by the devil and believe his lies, that the Lord isn't listening to us, and doesn't love us; just because He didn't answer our prayers and come to our rescue *within a 24-hour period*. That's just not true! There's a story in the Bible about a boy who was demon possessed, but the disciples couldn't cast the demon out. After Jesus drove out the demon, His disciples asked Him why they couldn't drive out the demon. He answered, *"This kind cannot be driven out by anything but prayer and fasting."* (see Mark 9:20-29) In the same sense, some things cannot come out of us, *except through hoping and expecting, while waiting*! In other words, some things *cannot be developed in us*, except by being *steadfast* or *stout-hearted*!

We've got to be *balanced* in our thinking. This requires strength and *courage*. This means that we can't become fearful. God has not called us to be cowards, or *"given us a spirit of fear."* Instead, He instills – *"... [He has given us a spirit] of power and of love and of sound judgment and personal discipline [abilities that result in a calm, well-balanced mind and self-control]."* (2 Timothy 1:7) Therefore, we must stand still and be *"stout."*

The Hebrew word for *"stout"* is *amats* (aw-mats). It means to be "alert, bold, courageous, determined, established, fortified, hardened, strong" and "<u>steadfastly minded</u>." I really like that last one! When we have a stout heart, we move ahead boldly and courageously, while being mindful that no matter what or who we encounter that opposes us; *"we are more than conquerors"* (see Romans 8:37), because *"He Who lives in you is greater (mightier) than he"* who opposes you! (see 1 John 4:4) When our heart is conditioned this way, we experience more conquests, than we will experience being confused, cowardly, and conquered.

We can't experience consistent victories and constantly accomplish our assignments without continually being *well-balanced*. This requires discipline and diligence. This is why we're commanded, *"Be <u>well balanced</u> (temperate, sober of mind), be vigilant and cautious <u>at all times</u>; for that enemy of yours, the devil, roams around like a lion roaring [in fierce hunger], <u>seeking someone to seize upon and devour</u>. Withstand him; <u>be firm in faith</u> [against his onset – rooted, <u>established</u>, strong, <u>immovable</u>, and determined], knowing that the same (identical) sufferings* *are appointed to your brotherhood (the whole body of Christians] throughout the world."* (1 Peter 5:8-9 emphasis added)

Because our enemy is incessantly seeking us, we must be consistently careful. Every Believer has a responsibility to remain *cautious constantly*, even though we have and *Ever-Present Help* with us. He is there to strengthen and establish us, so that when the adversary attempts to *"seize upon and devour"* us, we are able to *"withstand"* him! That's because what the devil doesn't want to deal with, is a *"determined"* disciple of Jesus Christ! When we are resting in and submitted to Him, satan doesn't stand a chance against us! *"So then, surrender to God. Stand up to the devil and resist him and he will turn and run away from you."* (James 4:7 TPT)

Having balanced thinking means that we don't feel defeated, because *we think we're the only ones* being attacked or under pressure. In some cases, it's not an attack, it's an *appointment*! Therefore, we must remember that we're not the only ones engaged in warfare, and remain *steadfast* – resolving to withstand the attacks, and advance forward, knowing that God will fortify and establish us, as we wait on Him. What helps, is following the direction of Psalmist David, who wrote, *"So cheer up! Take courage all you who love him. Wait for him to break through for you, all you who trust him!"* (Psalm 31:24 TPT)

Sometimes, during the process, we may have to perform a *balancing act* in our minds. We must acknowledge that we're aware of the adversary's position, while also asserting that we are *alert to God's Presence*, and acquainted with His command: *"Stay alert! I am God, the God of everything living. Is there anything I can't do?"* (Jeremiah

32:27 MSG) When we're alert or aware of this, we acknowledge that He is able to do *"anything"* – if we *"are able to believe, all things are possible to the believer"*, then we will see it come to pass (see Mark 9:23 TPT).

Because we believe, and in fact, *know* that *"all things are possible"* to us, and we also *"know that all things work together for good to those who love God"* (see Romans 8:28), we must always hold on to these promises, and use them as the weights or a *counterbalance* when the enemy comes to knock us off balance! In order to achieve this, we must remain alert. Because the Lord knew that this was essential to our survival and success, He wasn't satisfied with the Apostle Peter's command to us to be *"<u>well balanced</u> (temperate, sober of mind), be vigilant..."* So, He sanctioned Peter's peer, Paul, to plead differently.

The Apostle Paul pleaded, *"Be alert and on your guard; <u>stand firm in your faith</u> (your conviction respecting man's relationship to God in divine things, keeping the trust and holy fervor born of faith and a part of it). Act like men and be courageous; <u>grow in strength</u>! Let everything you do <u>be done in love</u> (true love to God and man as inspired by God's love for us)."* (1 Corinthians 16:13-14 emphasis added)

We are to *always* be on alert and on guard. However, besides being on high alert externally, we must be equally attentive, *internally*! In other words, *"Keep and guard your heart with all vigilance and above all that you guard, for out of it flow the springs of life."* (Proverbs 4:23) Other translations read, *"So above all, guard the affections of your heart, for they affect all that you are. Pay attention to <u>the welfare of your innermost being</u>, for from there flows the wellspring of life."* (TPT emphasis added), *"Carefully guard*

It's All We Can Eat!

your thoughts because they are the source of true life." (CEV), *"Be careful how you think; your life is shaped by your thoughts."* (GNT), *"...that's where life starts."* (MSG), *"...for it determines the course of your life."* (NLT), *"...because the source of your life flows from it."* (GWT), *"...for it is the source of life's consequences."* (CJB)

Because the adversary knows that the battle ground is in the mind, he seeks out and goes after those who have an *unbalanced and unguarded* mind. In order to avoid becoming his victim, we must be vigilant and well-balanced in our thinking! If we're not sober-minded, diligent, and guarding our heart, we will suffer consequences that we can't possibly calculate or comprehend.

In order to handle the pressure and press forward, through the process that God has us in, *protecting our heart must be a high priority*! As a man thinks in his heart, so is he. (see Proverbs 23:7) If we think we're defeated, we will be. But if we think *we are more than conquerors*, God is with us, and that He will strengthen us, sustain us, and cause our hearts to be *steadfast* or *stout*; we will be! This requires maturity. We've got to *man-up*, and become mighty men and virtuous women of God.

Concerning maturity, Apostle Paul wrote, *"Act like men and be courageous; grow in strength!"* It's interesting that immediately afterwards, he wrote, *"Let everything you do be done in love (true love to God and man as inspired by God's love for us)."* The Passion Translation and The Message respectively read, *"Let love and kindness be the motivation behind all that you do." "Keep your eyes open, hold tight to your convictions, give it all you've got, be resolute, and love without stopping."* (1 Corinthians 16:13-

14 emphasis added) Included in the *"everything"* and the *"all"* is being *alert, steadfast,* and *well-balanced.*

However, this is not possible without love. When I read that verse above, I heard the Holy Spirit say, "*Love is needed* to develop steadfastness." As I wrote in a previous chapter, His love for us liberates us, and *our love for Him* keeps us liberated! This is why everything we do, should be done in love. It's a *necessity*! I reminded of the hit song by Stevie Wonder, *Love's In Need of Love Today*. As profound as the title is, the lyrics are equally as profound and powerful! In the same way that "hate's goin' 'round, breakin' many hearts", our enemy, the adversary is looking for someone to assign his *surveillance team* to – someone *not* sober-minded, but unbalanced, undisciplined, and unloving – he's "<u>seeking someone to seize upon and devour.</u>"

My point is that God is Love, and in order for the love He has already deposited in us to develop steadfastness to be effective, we need to demonstrate our love and affection for Him, by always being alert, guarding our hearts, holding tight to our hope and convictions, and trusting in Him. We must trust in Him with all of our hearts and affectionately acknowledge Him in all of our ways, instead of leaning to our own understanding, is *an act of love.*

It's All We Can Eat! Let's Love Steadfastly!

Chapter 10
Guarded & Guided By Godliness

"...and in [exercising] steadfastness [develop] godliness (piety),"

There's No Such Thing As A Free Lunch!

Whether you say, "There's no such thing as a free lunch." or "There ain't no such thing as a free lunch!", the message is still the same: whatever goods or services are provided to us, someone has to pay for them. As my mom used to say, "You can't get something for *nothing*!" She also instilled in me, that anything worth having – anything of value, had to be earned or should be worked for. Someone else, who had the same sentiment was King David.

When King David was in distress, because of the pestilence upon the land, he went to up to the threshing floor of Araunah, to build an altar to the Lord and make a sacrifice to Him. When Araunah asked why he was there, King David told him about his desire – his purpose was to purchase some of his property; his threshing floor, so that he could build an altar to the Almighty, and pray so that the plague would dissipate from the people. Araunah replied by not only offering to *give* him the threshing floor, but also the oxen for the sacrifice, as well as the yokes for wood to build the altar, and instruments to perform the service! However, in response to such an extravagant gift, David replied, *"No, but I will buy it of you for a price. I will not offer burnt offerings to the Lord my God of that which costs me nothing."* (see 2 Samuel 24:19-25)

The Message reads, *"No. I've got to but it from you for a good price; I'm not going to offer God, my God, sacrifices that are no sacrifice."* My point is that what was given to us, cost God something – He gave *"his one and only, unique Son as a gift."* (see John 3:16 TPT) Although salvation is a free gift to the world, it cost The Lord everything, to be our *Everything*! Therefore, we should realize that *"godliness"*, although given freely, should *cost us* something. We must invest in the impartation. We have a duty to do something with what's deposited in us. The piety implanted in us was purchased by Him. However, we must participate in its development. In other words, we must make some sacrifices for the *Sacrifice* that was made for us!

Sacrifice seems to be synonymous with insulting, to some people. We live in a world where some would like to believe and rather sing the song of a famous entertainer, who said, "I woke up like this." Sadly, some people thought it was as simple as singing a song, and this became their anthem. However, it's been my experience, and maybe yours too, that there have been *many lies told and believed*, because of the lyrics in songs! While on Earth, we may wake up *righteous and blameless* (because of His Sacrifice), we may even wake up blessed (because of His grace, mercy, and generosity), but we *never* wake up flawless! We must never deceive ourselves or allow others to deceive us into thinking that what we have and what we are to become, is effortless. No, it isn't – it comes with a price tag! There's a cost for the oil in our *"alabaster"* boxes (see John 12:3)!

The Gift Of Godliness

Godliness is a gift from God. However, it is also a gift that we are expected to give back to Him, as well as extend to others. The Greek word for *"godliness (piety)"* is *eusebeia* (yoo-seb-i-ah). It's "someone's inner, godly heart response to the things of God, which shows itself in reverence." It's devotion to God. However, it is devotion, as *determined* or *defined* by, God, and not our own determination of what devotion is. This reminds me of an old underwear TV commercial (available on YouTube). The premise and tagline were, "They don't say 'Hanes' until *I say*, 'They say 'Hanes!'" The "I" was the conscientious

It's All We Can Eat!

Inspector 12. We have our own Inspector, and our devotion or godliness isn't devotion or godliness – in fact, our love isn't love, unless *He* says it is!

Concerning godliness or piety, Apostle Peter wrote, *"Everything we could ever need for <u>life and complete devotion to God</u> has already been deposited in us by his divine power. For all this was lavished upon us through the rich experience of knowing him <u>who has called us by name and invited us to come to him</u> through a glorious manifestation of his goodness."* (2 Peter 1:3 TPT emphasis added)

His definition of devotion is one that displays or is a true reflection of His character. He has given us *"everything"* we need to devote ourselves to demonstrating His character to others, as well as delighting Him with our devotion and dedication to Him. This is what Apostle Paul wrote: *"Every spiritual blessing in the heavenly realm has already been lavished upon us as a love gift from our wonderful heavenly Father…"* (Ephesians 1:3 TPT)

Every spiritual blessing needed to bless others and demonstrate God's love, as well as bless and love God, has already been given to us, as a love gift from our Father. Everything needed to distribute *the fruit of the Spirit* has already been dispensed to and deposited in us. Our appropriate response should be to reciprocate with what we've received.

Everything means *everything*! You could also say, "Our Everything gave us *"everything"* we need to please Him, by becoming *"everything"* He called us to be!" Pivoting back to 2 Peter 1:3, other translations read, *"Everything that goes into a life of pleasing God has been miraculously given to us by getting to know, personally and intimately, the One who invited us to God. The best invitation we ever received!"* (MSG), *"...[absolutely] everything necessary for [a dynamic spiritual] life and godliness..."* (AMP), *"...everything that is necessary for living the truly good life..."* (Phillips), *"...everything we need to experience life and to reflect God's true nature..."* (Voice) Everything is *everything*! We have no excuses. I recently heard a successful businessman say, "Excuses only sound good to the person who uses them." So, I certainly won't attempt to type an excuse.

Trust me, I was also talking to *myself*, as I typed this! I am in no way, implying that this is easy, because at times, it isn't easy – at least for me. However, what helps us keep this commitment, in spite of challenges, is to commit it to prayer, and perhaps, make it a point of meditation. Apostle Paul told Timothy (and us), *"...that [outwardly] we may pass a quiet and undisturbed life [and inwardly] a peaceable one in all godliness and reverence in every way."* (1 Timothy 2:2) Paul was pleading for theirs and our prayers, intercessions, and petitions for those in *"positions of authority or high responsibility..."* However, we must never forget that we are also in *"positions of authority or high responsibility..."* Therefore, we must not neglect our responsibility to pray for ourselves in this manner, as well. We pray as fervently for ourselves, as we do for others. Or am I the only one who sometimes struggle with this?

This goes back to my point about godliness *costing* us something. It's going to cost time in intercession for others. It's going to cost seasons of sacrifice, as we fast. It's going to cost not participating in activities we enjoy, because we're somewhere, praying and petitioning for ourselves or someone else. The Passion Translation reads, *"...Pray for all men with all forms of prayers and requests as you intercede with intense passion."* (see 1 Timothy 2:1) It seems to me, like this should be seated in the category of *self-care* or *self-love*.

Another thing it will cost us is time and energy in training. We have to train ourselves, as well as receive training from those who are seasoned and skilled in areas where we aren't. However, we must take the initiative when it comes to training. *"Train yourself toward godliness (piety), [keeping yourself spiritually fit] ...godliness (spiritual training) is useful and of value in everything and in every way, for it holds promise for the present life and also for the life which is to come."* (see 1 Timothy 4:7-8)

Apostle Paul was admonishing Timothy (and us) to abstain or avoid fables, legends, myths, old wives tales, and senseless traditions. Instead, we are to be *"engaged in the training of truth that brings righteousness."* (TPT) Because of their substantial age difference, Paul often referred to Timothy as his son. He was old enough to be Timothy's father, if not grandfather. Timothy could have been seen or considered as a child. However, as I was writing this, I was reminded that we are to *"Train up a child in the way that he should go..."* (see Proverbs 22:6)

What I heard as I thought about that verse, was that we have to sometimes see ourselves, and humble ourselves, as a child, and get the training we need. We may even have to train *ourselves*. No matter where, or from whom we get our training, it's our responsibility to get it, and it must be based in *"godliness."* It should be *"...the sound and wholesome messages of our Lord Jesus Christ (the Messiah) and teaching which is in agreement with godliness (piety toward God),"* (see 1 Timothy 6:3) It's teaching founded on the fact and the time-tested truth, that the *"holy awe of God"* (godliness) is of the utmost importance. (TPT)

Godliness must be our *passionate pursuit*. We are to aggressively *"...aim at and pursue righteousness (right standing with God and true goodness), godliness (which is the loving fear of God and being Christlike), faith, love, steadfastness (patience), and gentleness of heart."* (1 Timothy 6:11) While vacationing in the Dominican Republic, I spent some time on the archery range at the resort. I learned very quickly, that hitting the "bull's eye" isn't as easy or effortless, as it looks! Acquiring such skill doesn't happen accidently – it requires awareness, focus, patience, intentionality, as well as concentrated and concerted effort.

I had no idea that an afternoon activity, such as archery lessons would one day, serve as a reminder of the cost or *requirement of godliness*. You see, archery isn't just a matter of picking up a bow, an arrow, and pointing at the target. There are essentials, which must be acquired and implemented, in order to be effective in hitting the target in the center. You can't just master one of the essentials. There's an assortment of them, which must all be engaged seemingly simultaneously, such as stance, grip, posture, bow arm, anchor point, release, and follow-through.

In the same way that we need to implement an assortment of essentials, in order to be skillful in archery, we also need an *assortment of essentials* in order to add to our faith and *"godliness"* as well as supplement our necessary training. Therefore, we must *persevere* in our pursuit of training. That's why were told, *"So don't lose a minute in <u>building on</u> what you've been given, <u>complementing</u> your* *basic faith with good character, spiritual understanding, alert discipline, passionate patience, reverent wonder, warm friendliness, and <u>generous love, each dimension fitting into and developing the others</u>.*" (2 Peter 1:5-7 MSG emphasis added)

Godliness guides us in how we conduct ourselves. It arrests our attention and raises our awareness of what real reverence of Him is, and *"…what kind of person ought [each of] you to be [in the meanwhile] in consecrated and holy behavior and devout and godly qualities, While you wait and earnestly long for (expect and hasten) the coming day of God…"* (see 2 Peter 3:11-12) When we are in *"holy awe of God"* guidance is the outgrowth. In other words, when we acknowledge God in all of our ways, what grows, reveals itself or appears in response to our acknowledgement; is guidance (see Proverbs 3:5-6).

Concerning conducting ourselves, our reverence of Him will reveal itself in how we respond to Him, how we relate to others, and in our daily routine – how we teach or *train* ourselves. In other words, our piety is proven by how we *press* into our training and preparation. In order to ensure that his preparation was *profitable*, the Apostle was persistent. He wrote, *"Now every athlete who goes into training conducts himself temperately and restricts himself in all things. They do it to win a wreath that will soon wither, but we [do it to receive a crown of eternal blessedness] that cannot wither."* (1 Corinthians 9:25) *"A true athlete will be disciplined in every respect, practicing self-control…"* (TPT)

His perspective on how we are to prepare and put into practice, our piety is on point. As I alluded to earlier, the implication is *not* that it's easy. However, it is necessary and possible. Next, Paul makes his point *personal*. Concerning conduct, he continues, *"Therefore I do not run uncertainly (without definite aim). I do not box like one beating the air and striking without an adversary. But [like a boxer] I buffet my body [handle it roughly, discipline it by hardships] and subdue it, for fear that proclaiming to others the Gospel and things pertaining to it, I myself should become unfit [not stand the test, be unapproved and rejected as a counterfeit]."* (1 Corinthians 9:26-27) *"…I don't run just for exercise or box like one throwing aimless punches, but I train like a champion athlete. I subdue my body and get it under my control…"* (TPT emphasis added)

Whether you've eye witnessed a champion athlete train, watched an actor train for a movie role or portray an athlete in training (movies like Rocky or Creed), or maybe you, yourself were a champion athlete; I'm sure that you'll agree that there's some *rigorous* training involved. The same energy and intense effort to train this way, should be the same energy that we should exert, as we train in righteousness and walk or engage in *"godliness."* As we submit ourselves to Him, He strengthens us to subdue our bodies.

Godliness was purchased for and implanted in us to *profit* us. Pertaining to the profitability of *godliness*, the Apostle Paul told Timothy (and us), *"[And it is, indeed, a source of immense profit, for] godliness accompanied with contentment (that contentment which is a sense of inward sufficiency) is great and abundant gain."* (1 Timothy 6:6 emphasis added) This counsel was given in contrast to the controversial belief of those with corrupt minds – those robbed of the truth, *"who imagine that godliness or righteousness is a source of profit [a money-making business, a means of livelihood]."* We were warned to withdraw from such. (see 1 Timothy 6:5)

The Greek word for *"gain"* is *porismos* (por-is-mos). It means "a providing, a means of gain." Its origin is from the word *porizo*, which means "to procure" or acquire for oneself. Properly, porismos means "a specific way (route) that brings gain or profit." As I was studying this word, the Holy Spirit reminded me of Matthew 16:26 which reads, *"For what will it profit a man if he gains the whole world and forfeits his life [his blessed life in the kingdom of God]? Or what would a man give as an exchange for his [blessed] life [in the kingdom of God]?"*

There's *nothing* we can acquire, do, exchange, or procure on our own, that compares to what we can gain from God! However, this blessed life in the Kingdom of God is secured by being *specific* and *intentional*. In other words, there are requirements regarding the routes, ways, and roads we take. We are informed, *"But the gate is narrow (contracted by pressure) and the way is straightened and compressed that leads away to life, and few are those who find it."* (Matthew 7:14) In contrast to the narrowness, contracting pressure and compression, our focus must be on contentment with the prescribed course or way of life.

The Greek word for *"contentment"* is *autarkeia* (ow-tar-ki-ah). It means "self-satisfaction, self-sufficiency." Properly, for the Spirit-filled Christian, it means *having all they need within* through the indwelling Christ." To me, it's as if having this state of mind or sufficiency *magnifies* whatever it is that we have or possess. Some translations of Matthew 16:26 substitute the word *"life"* with the word *"soul."* When we are content, our soul – the seat of our affections is *satisfied*.

It's All We Can Eat!

What those unrighteous ones either didn't realize or refused to believe, was that there's an *abundance* of blessings, benefits, and profit – great gain, in *"godliness"* and righteousness! We're encouraged to be content in this, and cautioned, *"Let your character or moral disposition be free from love of money [including greed, avarice, lust, and craving for earthly possessions] and be <u>satisfied with your present</u> [circumstances and with what you have];"* (Hebrews 13:5a emphasis added) What we're cautioned against is the love – more specifically, the *"lust"* for money. God doesn't have a problem with us acquiring money and accumulating wealth. In fact, I believe that He's even more pleased when we can *multiply* it! His problem – what He commands against, is *coveting* and *lusting* for it! He doesn't mind us having it, as long as *it doesn't have us*!

What's more beneficial than the monetary gains we make or get, or the financial wealth accumulated, is the *contentment and satisfaction* with what we already have. What, or more accurately, *Who* we have is priceless because He is *Everything* we need! You can't put a price tag on Him. We are told, *"for He [God] Himself has said, I will not in any way fail you nor give you up nor leave you without support. [I will] not, [I will] not in any degree leave you helpless nor forsake nor let [you] down (relax My hold on you)! [Assuredly not!]"* (Hebrews 13:5b)

This is by far, my *favorite* Bible verse! Wow, what a benefits package! Nothing can compare with the Presence promotion, protection, , provision, partnership and support of God! There's a satisfaction of the soul – such a peace and contentment that can't be calculated, all because The Greater One, the Personification of *"great gain"* is with us! Everything we need shows up with Him when He shows up.

It's All We Can Eat!

That's because *everything* we need is with and in Him. He is El Shaddai, The All-Mighty, and All-Sufficient One. When He appears, our needs disappear!

It's futile to attempt to try to figure it or Him out because we can't. *"His understanding is unsearchable"* (see Isaiah 40:28), and His great generosity, hospitality, and sufficiency are all a *mystery*. Along with those mysteries, is the mystery of *"godliness."* We are assured, *"And great and important and weighty, we confess, is the hidden truth (the mystic secret) of godliness..."* (1 Timothy 3:16) The Passion Translation reads, *"For the mystery of righteousness is truly amazing!"*

This *"mystery"* and *"righteousness"* written about, is Christ, in us. And because of our union, He is no longer a mystery to us. Because He is in us, we not only have *Hope*, so do others! We were rewarded and it has been revealed to us *"...the riches of the glory of this mystery, which is Christ within and among you, the Hope of [realizing the] glory."* (Colossians 1:26-27) So, since He resides within us, all of His riches and everything we need to be revealed to us, resides within us, as well! We just need to rest in Him, as we reverence Him. In doing so, we guard our hearts, for it is from this reservoir, that *"the issues of life"* – including righteousness and godliness, flow (see Proverbs 4:23).

Again, I'm not saying that this will be easy. However, it's much simpler when we don't attempt to do it in our own strength. We shouldn't allow ourselves to be deceived by the phrase, "I'm self-sufficient." None of us should *"estimate and think of himself more highly than he ought"* (see Romans 12:3). There is only One Who's Self-Sufficient, and He is *El Shaddai*. We are reminded, *"Not that we are fit (qualified and sufficient in ability) of* *ourselves...or count anything as coming from us, but <u>our power and ability and sufficiency are from God</u>.*" (2 Corinthians 3:5) *"Yet we don't see ourselves as capable enough to do anything in our own strength, <u>for our true competence flows from God's empowering presence</u>."* (TPT emphasis added)

There's so much security and stability in our humility. When we remind ourselves of our role, and respond with reverence to Him, it results in our capacity being enlarged or reimagined. Its' not so we can have more, just to *have* more or horde, but so that we can *give and serve* more! Although we are to humble ourselves as a child (see Matthew 18:3), sometimes we must take it a step further (or lower) and see ourselves as *jars of clay*. His expectation is that *"...the grandeur and exceeding greatness of the power may be shown to be from God and not from ourselves."* (2 Corinthians 4:7) *"We are like common clay jars that carry this glorious treasure within, so that the extraordinary overflow of power will be seen as God's not ours."* (TPT)

Clay jars. Pottery, or as described in the above verse, *"earthen vessels"* (KJV). That's how we should view ourselves. There's value and virtue within these vessels. Within our hearts, is *"... [the divine light of the Gospel]."* (2 Corinthians 4:7) Therefore, we must guard against damage or breakage – not only from others, but from ourselves, as well. Damage or breakage can occur, due to our dissatisfaction with how we were formed, displeasure with what we were fashioned to do, or our disrespect for the One Who formed, molded, fashioned, and made us.

We are warned, *"Woe to him who strives with his Maker!...Shall the clay say to him who fashions it, What do you think you are making? or, Your work has no handles?"*

It's All We Can Eat!

(see Isaiah 45:9) We have no say, in how we are shaped, because before we were a physical shape or form, our Potter *knew* us (see Jeremiah 1:5), what He wanted us to be, and how to make or shape us into it! So, instead of insisting on having a say so, we should just *serve what we have*, from who and what we *are*. That's called *submission*!

In the same way that more juice can be produced from fruit as it is squeezed, and more fruit can be produced from the tree that is pruned; we become more productive in serving others, and satisfying our Father (the Husbandman), when we submit ourselves to be squeezed, molded, shaped, and pruned. It's called *living God's way*.

It's "All We Can Eat!", Family. Let's Love Godly!

Chapter 11
Born To Love & Assigned To Affection

"And in exercising godliness [develop] brotherly affection..."

It's All We Can Eat!

In volume one of this book series, I began my introduction with Galatians 5:22-24, which is the foundational Scripture for the series. From *The Message*, it reads, *"But what happens when we live God's way?"* In my opinion, this could easily have been translated, "What happens when we have a lifestyle of godliness?" or "What would happen if we had a propensity to practice piety – what if our proclivity were to be in His Presence persistently?" Wow! What would our lives be like? Probably more importantly, what would our world be like?!

This reminded me of a song by Pastor Ben Tankard (along with Tribe of Benjamin), on his *Git Yo Praize On!* CD. The song is titled, *What Kinda World*. The lyrics are, "What kind of world would it be, if everyone was just like me? What kind of love would I see if what I gave came back to me?" That's deep! The song is only fifty-eight seconds long and is more of an interlude. However, the questions are so profound and thought-provoking! I stopped writing for a few seconds, to go listen to it on YouTube. I then, discovered that there's another song, from 1971, by The 21st Century Ltd., titled "What Kind of World Would This Be (If Ev'rybody In It Were Just Like Me)" That one is three minutes long and poses many questions that may have you asking yourself if you have the mind of Christ or if brotherly love and sisterly affection are your primary attributes. It certainly did so, to me!

Well, let's go back to the question in Galatians, and see what God has to say about what happens when we live *His* way: *"He brings gifts into our lives, much the same way that fruit appears in an orchard – things like affection for others..."* The first thing I noticed was that we're given the gift of *Love* or *the fruit of the Spirit,* and when He arrives,

It's All We Can Eat!

He brings an *arrangement* and assortment of *gifts* with Him! The reason I included the word arrangement is because there is a certain *order* and reason or purpose for how the gifts and fruit are presented to us. These gifts are *living, active, productive* gifts! One of the gifts or fruit that's produced is *affection*.

Regarding living *"God's way"* The Passion Translation reads, *"But the fruit produced by the Holy Spirit within you is divine love in all its varied expressions: joy that overflows, peace that subdues, patience that endures, kindness in action..."* (see Galatians 5:22-23) Actually, the Greek word for fruit can be translated "harvest." Also of importance, is the singular textual inference of *love* being the *fruit* or *harvest* of the Holy Spirit, with the various virtues (joy, peace, patience, kindness, etc.) being *expressions* or *displays* of that love. You've probably heard someone say, "Love is an *action* word." Here's an example of that statement.

This expression of love is *agape* (ag-ah-pay). It means "benevolence, charity, esteem," and "goodwill." It's the type of love which centers in moral preference. It's divine love – the God *quality*, or the love that God *prefers* – the *unconditional* love of God. Similar to altruism, it's devoted to, or *seeks the highest good* of others. It's not *feelings-focused*, nor based on attitude or emotion. This *expression* of love includes a *commitment to the welfare* or well-being of others without any conditions or circumstances. As stated, it means "goodwill." However, I'd like to think of it as *God's Will*! It's the love from which *all other* forms of love are birthed or *flow*.

Concerning *"kindness in action"* from the 2 Peter 1:7 perspective, as we practice *godliness*, we're required to add to or *"[develop] brotherly affection"* (AMPC), *"brotherly kindness"* (NIV), and *"add mercy towards your brothers and sisters"* (TPT). The Greek word for *"kindness"* is *philadelphia*, which means "brotherly love" or "love of the brethren." This is absolutely the love that *we should all aim at attaining*.

The English definition for affection is much different from the Biblical or Greek definition. At first, it caught me off guard. But because I've been studying this subject for some time now, it made more sense, after I studied a little more. From English, French, and Latin words, it is defined as "desire, inclination, wish, intention; an emotion of the mind, passion, lust as opposed to reason; disposition; love, attraction, enthusiasm." This was helpful. However, not nearly as helpful, and insightful as what I discovered, when I searched my Bible dictionary and Greek lexicon.

The Greek word used for *"affection"* is *crestotes* (khray-stot-ace). It means "goodness, excellence, uprightness" and is characterized by "kindness and gentleness." It is a noun derived from *xrestotes*, which means "useful, profitable." Properly, "useable i.e., well-fit for use (for what is really needed); kindness that is also serviceable." As Believers, this is the type of kindness that is *useful*. It meets real needs, the way God would meet them, with the timing God would meet them. It's serving or fulfilling a need in the same fashion that The Father would. It can be described as a "divine kindness." It's Spirit-produced goodness and gentleness that meets the needs of humanity, without harshness.

I thought I was done with this subject. However, the next day, after writing the above portion of this chapter, I was prompted to dig a little deeper. As I stated earlier, this *brotherly love* and *sisterly affection* are attributes that we should all *aim at attaining*. When I looked again, in my

It's All We Can Eat!

Strong's Complete Dictionary of Bible Words, I saw something else. You see, the Greek word *philadelphia* is also defined as "fraternal affection." Fraternal is from the Latin word, *fraternus*. It means "friendly, closely allied," literally "brotherly."

When I wrote fraternal, I had an interesting thought. The thought was that in the same way fraternal twins are the result of the same pregnancy and share their genes; we, as Believers share a *similar experience*! Although we look different, and are not the same gender, we are the result of the *same pregnancy* – we are all *"born of the Spirit"* (see John 3:3-8). We have received or experienced what Jesus told Nicodemus was *required* to live in The Kingdom, when He told him, *"Before a person can perceive God's kingdom realm, they must first <u>experience a rebirth</u>."* (TPT emphasis added) We also share the *same genes* – we have Divine DNA, because we are *"born of God"* (see John 1:12-13)! HALLELUJAH!!!

Digging deeper, I saw the Greek words *philanthropia*, which is "fondness of mankind, i.e. benevolence (philanthropy)." I also saw the word *philanthropos*, which means "fondly to man (philanthropically) i.e. humanely: – courteously." I found out that in order to fulfill our responsibility as Kingdom Citizens, we're required to display *brotherly love* and *sisterly affection* by demonstrating *benevolence* or *fondness* of mankind – treating them *courteously, humanely*, and generously. These words are related to *phileo*, which denotes personal attachment, and means "to approve of, befriend, welcome, show signs of love" and "treat affectionately." Long story short: We're *all* called to be *Philanthropists!*

It's All We Can Eat!

It's "All We Can Eat!", Family. Let's Love Philanthropically!

Chapter 12
Love Like The Lord

"And in exercising brotherly affection [develop] Christian love..."
(2 Peter 1:7b)

It's All We Can Eat!

The night before beginning this chapter, I read 1 Peter 1:7 from the NIV, which reads, *"and to brotherly kindness, love."* I then, cross-referenced it with the verses below, and I was blown away, by what I read! Because I've been studying Biblical love or *God's brand of love*, since writing volume 1, and this volume, up to this chapter; I thought I had a sufficient understanding of God's *brand* or *quality* of love. On the surface, *"love"* seemed to be a simple *supplement* to *"brotherly kindness."* However, although I've read all three verses many times, in various versions, I was both, surprised and *stirred* by what I saw and sensed, after reading them this time.

On the morning of my writing session for this chapter, I viewed my Facebook Memories for this day, ten years ago (01/20/12), I posted, "Good Morning FBF. It's 'Fervelicious Friday!' Be Fervent. Stay On Fire!" I included the following passage of Scripture: *"Be kindly affectioned one to another with brotherly love; in honour preferring one another; Not slothful in business; fervent in spirit; serving the Lord; Rejoicing in hope; patient in tribulation; continuing instant in prayer; Distributing to the necessity of saints; given to hospitality. Bless them which persecute you: bless, and curse not. Rejoice with them that do rejoice, and weep with them that weep."* (Romans 12:10-15 KJV)

For the record, I'm well-aware that *fervelicious* won't be found in the Webster's Dictionary. I have a habit of making up words, and I've made a hobby out of developing my own dictionary with them. So, *fervelicious* is a word I formed, as I studied the text; especially verse eleven. So, 10 years after that Facebook post, I found myself reading what seemed to be an unfamiliar verse – this time, from a different version. There I was, reading, *"Be devoted to one another with [authentic] brotherly affection [as members of one family], give preference to one another in honor; never lagging behind in diligence; aglow in the*

Spirit, enthusiastically serving the Lord;" (Romans 12:10-11 AMP)

The Greek word for *"devoted"* is philostorgos (fil-os-tor-gos). It is defined as "tenderly loving." It means "family affection, natural or family love", and "lover of family." For the Believer, it's that special affection shared between members of God's family – us, who are born-again, because we believed in and received The *Son*, we were *adopted* by and *serve* the same *Father*.

The Greek word for *"authentic"* is *alethenos* (al-ay-thee-nos). It's defined as "true" and means "made of truth." It can also mean "real, genuine; emphasizing the organic connection (authentic unity) between what is true and it's source or origin." As Believers, we know and are untied to The One Who is True. He is the Real Source and Authentic Origin of Life. In a world of false and counterfeit, He is The Only Connection for a life that flourishes! We know He is Faithful and True, because real recognizes Real! As family members, we're required to *keep it real* with one another. Just as we are connected to Christ, authenticity or *authentic unity* keeps us connected to each other. This requires transparency, or in urban vernacular, *keeping it 100!*

Along with transparency, *"honor"* is also required. Other translations of this verse read, *"...giving <u>precedence and showing honor to one another</u>."* (AMPC), *"Outdo one another in showing honor..."* (ESV), *"...take <u>delight in honoring</u> each other."* (NLT) The Greek word for *"preference"* is proegemomai (pro-ay-geh-om-ahee). It's defined as "to go before (as a leader)." The thought is "I lead onward by example, go before, prefer." Properly, it means "to lead the way, passing on the right example (modeling, exhibiting) the proper behavior, i.e. so others can follow the one "going first." In this current "Me first!" culture, it's

It's All We Can Eat!

refreshing to be reminded of what the *proper motive* for being or going *first* is.

How About A Head Start?

The Greek word for *"precedence"* is provadisma. It means "priority, seniority" and "leading-edge." Another meaning is "head start." I like that one, because it reminded me of my childhood. My older family members or friends would give me a head start when we raced. They did this because they were bigger or faster, and they either wanted me to think I was going to win, or at least, make the race more competitive. They would do something similar when we played basketball. Sometimes, they would let me win – even though they knew they were better than me! It also reminded me of when my niece and nephew, as well as my sons were younger, and we would race. I would give them a head start, and as I caught up to them, I'd slow down to either tie or usually, let them win. I took the same approach, when playing basketball. Sometimes, I would intentionally miss the winning or tying shot, so that they could win.

Just reminiscing about those times – the smiles and laughter had me smiling! It also reminded me that this is how our Father expects us to treat our (spiritually) younger, and less mature siblings. As the older, more mature family members, our Father wants to see us consistently giving our younger siblings the *leading-edge* or head starts – we're supposed to *let them win*! It's what was meant by the instructions *"...each esteeming the other as more excellent than themselves;"* (Philippians 2:3 DBT) *"...let each regard the others <u>as better than</u> and superior to himself [thinking more highly of one another than you do of yourselves] ...each <u>for the interests of others</u>."* (see Philippians 2:3-4 AMPC emphasis added)

I now, realize that in the same way that my more mature friends and family members would let me outrun

155

them, and I would allow my younger family members to outrun me; we're required to let our spiritual family members *outrun* us. It's also our duty – our *devotion* should be to *outdo* each other! Not in a dishonorable or haughty way, but in an honorable and humble way. We're encouraged, *"Be devoted to tenderly loving your fellow believers as members of one family. Try to <u>outdo yourselves in respect and honor of one another</u>."* (Romans 12:10 TPT emphasis added)

That reminds me of the questions from the previous chapter: "What kind of world would it be, if everyone was just like me? What kind of love would I see if what I gave came back to me?" Can you imagine what life would be like, if we had a *lifestyle of outdoing and outrunning ourselves in respect and honor of one another*? I mean, what would the world look like, if we really *loved like the Lord*?!

W.J.W.D. (What Jesus Would Do?)

Those questions reminded me of another question. Back in the 1990s, there were a lot of wristbands and t-shirts sold in the U.S. that carried the message, "W.W.J.D. (What Would Jesus Do?)." I know both, what He would *do*, and also what He would *be*! He would be *passionate*! The Greek word for passionate is *pathema* (path-ay-mah). It means "suffering, affliction, emotion, an undergoing, an enduring." It also means "the capacity and privilege of experiencing strong feeling, deep emotion." It can also mean "fiery, flaming, glowing, aglow." Because He did it, His expectation is that we emulate Him. That's why we're commanded, *"Never lag in zeal and in earnest endeavor; <u>be aglow and burning with the Spirit</u>, serving the Lord."* (Romans 12:11 emphasis added)

What I heard, when I read that verse, was that when we *"Outdo one another in showing honor"* we are *"serving the Lord."* When we *"esteem"* each other, we *exemplify*

It's All We Can Eat!

Christ. When we "lead onward by example, go before, prefer" others; we let our *"light so shine"* in such a way, that others get to *"glorify God"* (see Matthew 5:16)! That's why we must be persistently passionate, remembering to *"Be enthusiastic to serve the Lord, <u>keeping your passion toward him boiling hot</u>! <u>Radiate with the glow of the Holy Spirit</u> and let him fill you with excitement as you serve him."* (Romans 12:11 TPT emphasis added) The NLT reads, *"Never be lazy, but work hard..."* with the footnote: "Or *but serve the Lord with a zealous spirit;* or *but let the Spirit excite you as you serve the Lord."*

In the afternoon of my writing session for this chapter, something else of significance occurred. It was the Inauguration of President Joseph R. Biden, Jr., and Vice President Kamala D. Harris. Besides being an answered prayer and historical, on so many levels; there was a message that emerged from a young lady, who *confirmed some of the content* that the Holy Spirit spoke to me, concerning this chapter! Without any advanced knowledge of her appearance, or the message that would emanate from her, The Holy Spirit had already written upon my heart, the need for unity, preference, community, precedence, respect, honor, esteeming each other, and thinking more highly of the interests of one another.

That afternoon, National Youth Poet Laureate, Amanda Gorman, in her poem, *The Hill We Climb*, in her own, inimitable way; illustrated and gave a call to action, to our country to collectively construct a better country, and by example, build a better world! One of the many lines that caught my attention was when she called upon us "To compose a country committed to all cultures, colors, characters, and conditions of man." As you might imagine, I momentarily asked myself, "What kind of world would this be?"

That's the world that we should be striving to construct. One that she called, "a union with purpose." This is the kind of mindset we must have, and union that ushers joy to our Father. We are commanded, *"Fill up and <u>complete my joy by living in harmony</u> and being of the same mind <u>and one in purpose</u>, having the <u>same love</u>, being in full accord and of <u>one harmonious mind and intention</u>." "...be joined together <u>in perfect unity</u> – <u>with one heart</u>, <u>one passion</u>, and <u>united in love</u>. Walk together with <u>one harmonious purpose</u> and you will fill my heart with <u>unbounded joy</u>."* (Philippians 2:2 emphasis added, TPT included) When we walk in love and unity as a family, we not only bring our Father joy, but we also experience it, and bring joy to the world!

One Mind, One Heart, One Purpose, One Love

When we have this *"same mind"* and are *"united in love"* and committed to constructing or composing this type of community; we won't waste time looking for what's wrong with others, nor will we be wary of their weapons, or weaponize our words. Instead, as Amanda asserted, we will "Lay down our arms so we can reach out our arms to one another." I know that this is the heart of our Heavenly Father, because it is written to us, *"Finally, all [of you] should be of <u>one and the same mind</u> [united in spirit], <u>sympathizing</u> [with one another], <u>loving</u> [each other] <u>as brethren</u> [of one household], <u>compassionate and courteous</u> (tenderhearted and humble)."* (1 Peter 3:8 emphasis added)

As I stated above, this is the heart of our Heavenly Father. However, what's in or on His heart isn't as impactful, until it reaches the hearts of humanity. One of the favorite hashtags or popular words on social media and in pop culture is "goals." Whether they're fitness goals, relationship goals, financial goals, etc.; everyone seems to have them, and are unashamed to show us. Here's one of our Heavenly Father's relationship goals for all of us: *"<u>Now, this is the goal</u>: to <u>live</u>*

<u>in harmony</u> with one another and <u>demonstrate affectionate love</u>, sympathy, and kindness towards other believers. <u>Let humility describe who you are as you dearly love one another</u>." (1 Peter 3:8 TPT emphasis added)

Once we agree to such lofty, but attainable goals, we can make *amazingly* great advancements! However, along with such an agreement, there must be a *greater sense of urgency* – a sense of urgence that Dr. Martin Luther King, Jr. recited, and President Barak Obama reiterated: "the fierce urgency of now." Long before these lauded, legendary Leaders launched such an illustrious concept into our lives, we were encouraged, *"But I urge and entreat you, brethren, by the name of the Lord Jesus Christ, that all of you <u>be in perfect harmony and full agreement</u> in what you say, and that there be no dissensions or factions or divisions among you, but that you <u>be perfectly united in your common understanding and in your opinions and judgements</u>."* (1 Corinthians 1:10 emphasis added)

We're called to walk together in *agreement*. The forefathers of this country desired to form a "more perfect union." That's an admirable goal – a commendable attempt to be committed to being on one accord. However, there was a major flaw with their effort, that's revealed in a question found in the Bible. It was asked, *"Do two walk together except they make an appointment and have agreed?" "Can two people walk together without agreeing on the direction?" "Do people walk hand in hand if they aren't going to the same place?"* (Amos 3:3 AMPC, NLT, MSG respectively)

Unless we first agree that the only *perfect union* is our common, collective, and consistent connection with Christ, The Prince of Peace; we will continue in uncertainty, unaccompanied, unassisted, and unable to become who and what we were called to be. Ultimately, we will remain weak and undone. The answer is *change*. This requires us moving away from our old, "Me first!" mindset, and be the first to extend *mercy*. In other words, we must have *giving others a head start* high on our list of priorities. We must also be willing to admire the strengths and might of others, and seek ways to combine our strengths, in order to compose or construct a better country and global community. I believe this is what Amanda meant, when she said, "If we merge mercy with might, and might with right, then love becomes our legacy and change, our birthright."

Therefore, in agreement and with a greater sense of urgency, we must endeavor to *"...agree to live in unity with one another and put to rest any division that attempts to tear you apart. Be restored as one united body living in perfect harmony. Form a consistent choreography among yourselves, having common perspective with shared values."* (1 Corinthians 1:10 TPT emphasis added) In order for us to experience breakthrough, we must be brave enough to breakdown whatever is attempting to tear or break us apart. To do so, requires us to recognize our diversity and differences as sources of strength and resources for recovery that should be respected, instead of reasons to disrespect or show disdain.

God has assigned us to the *"ministry of reconciliation"* (see 2 Corinthians 5:18), and appointed us as a *"repairer of the breach."* It was prophesied, *"And your ancient ruins shall be rebuilt; you shall raise up the foundations of [buildings that have laid waste for] many generations; and you shall be called Repairer of the Breach, Restorer of Streets to Dwell In."* (Isaiah 58:12) Although this was originally written about Jerusalem, I hope that you can see the spiritual application to our country (USA), and your city, town, community, and family. There are some systems, mindsets and structures that are in ruins and *"have laid waste"* for generations. Therefore, the appropriate response for us is to rebuild, reconcile, recover, repair, and restore.

The proper response will result in something very profitable for us. Part of the precondition of the promise is, *"And if you pour out that with which you sustain your own life for the hungry and satisfy the need of the afflicted, <u>then shall your light rise in darkness</u>, and your obscurity and gloom <u>become like noonday</u>."* (Isaiah 58:10) Illuminating light is available and waiting for us if we're willing to meet the conditions. As Amanda Gorman so graciously stated, "For there is always light, if only we're brave enough to see it, if only we're brave enough to be it."

There is so much that can be accomplished, if we do what Jesus did, and what He expects us to do. However, it requires courage and bravery. If we're willing to embrace the concepts that love conquers all – that we are *"more than conquerors"* (see Romans 8:37), and we're willing to do the work to rebuild; then, we may very well, witness what Amanda spoke of, when she said, "So, while once we asked, how could we possibly prevail over catastrophe? Now we assert, how could catastrophe possibly prevail over us?" This reminds me of when the Apostle Paul pondered, *"What then shall we say to [all] this? If God is for us, who [can be] against us? [Who can be our foe, if God is on our side?]"* (Romans 8:31)

Powerful and thought-provoking words. Words that prompt me to ask, "How could catastrophe, chaos, or confusion possibly conquer us?" Especially when we were encouraged, *"But no weapon that is formed against you shall prosper, and every tongue that shall rise against you in judgement you shall show to be in the wrong. This [peace, righteousness, security, triumph over opposition] is the heritage of the servants of the Lord [those in whom the ideal Servant of the Lord is reproduced]; this is the righteousness or the vindication which they obtain from Me [this is that which I impart to them as their justification], says the Lord."* (Isaiah 54:17)

When I read that, what stuck out was that The Lord always showed those who rose up in judgement against Him, to be wrong. He also walked in peace, righteousness, security, and triumphed over His enemies and overcame obstacles and opposition. If we love like the Lord loved, we can also live like the Lord lived. We're commanded to be *"imitators of God"* and to *"walk in love, [esteeming and delighting in one another] as Christ loved us…"* (Ephesians 5:1-2) This is our receipt – it reveals that He is *"reproduced"* in us. It's also evidence of the *"justification"* and *"vindication"* that *God imparted* to us!

The Power Of The Same Love

As I stated in the previous paragraph, if we love like the Lord loved, we can also live like the Lord lived. He not only left us a lifestyle that was legendary – it was a lifestyle of *legacy*! This is because He was *"reproduced"* in us. Therefore, the proper response is to do what He did: live like He lived, which requires that we *love* like He loved. Because we're a reproduction of Him, we are qualified and authorized to lead, live, and love with the same love that the Lord leads, lives, and loves with. We may not be able to duplicate Him, but we can certainly *replicate* Him.

Our *identity* in Christ is all that's required to release our power to replicate His love. Rich are the rewards we receive because of our obedient response. We are encouraged, *"And may the Lord make you to increase and excel and overflow in love for one another and for all people, just as we also do for you."* (1 Thessalonians 3:12 emphasis added) These words could have easily come audibly and directly from the mouth of God to us, individually. I say this, because the love He, our Father, wants us to have for each

It's All We Can Eat!

other is the *same love* He has for His Son and His Holy Spirit. It is also the same love They have for Him! Yes, He loves us *just like* He loves Them!

This became even more clearer to me, as I viewed various versions of the above verse: *"May the Lord make your love increase and overflow for each other and for everyone else, just as ours does for you."* (NIV) *"And may the Lord increase your love until it overflows toward one another and for all people, just as our love overflows toward you."* (TPT) *"May God our Father himself and our Master Jesus clear the road to you! And may the Master pour on the love so it fills your lives and splashes over on everyone around you, just as it does from us to you."* (MSG)

We should never confuse *same* with either; similar, complacent, idle, inert, or stagnant. Our Heavenly Father's expectation is that we take the *same love* – the abounding, *always-excelling, ever-increasing, overflowing love* that He has for His Son and His Holy Spirit, and that They have for Him; and love our brothers and sisters in the family of God, as well as everyone else – just as He does (or They do) for us! Wow, this reminds me of that song, *I Love You More Today, Than Yesterday, (But Not As Much As Tomorrow)*!

This love – this *"power that is at work within us, is able to [carry out His purpose and] do superabundantly, far over and above all that we [dare] ask or think [infinitely beyond our highest prayers, desires, hopes, and dreams –"* (Ephesians 3:20) We may never accurately or adequately imagine *"the great magnitude of the astonishing love of Christ in all its dimensions."* It is described as *"deeply intimate and far-reaching."* It was exclaimed, *"How <u>enduring and inclusive</u> it is! <u>Endless love beyond measurement</u> that transcends our understanding – this <u>extravagant love</u> pours into you until you are <u>filled to</u>*

It's All We Can Eat!

overflowing with the fullness of God!" (see Ephesians 3:18-20, emphasis added, TPT included)

His gift of love is truly "the gift that keeps on giving!" We have this life and the life to come, to attempt to comprehend *"how wide, how long, how high, and how deep His love is."* (see Ephesians 3:18 NLT) Therefore, our love should *keep giving*. The Father and Son, with Their love, has cleared the road for us. They have breached every boarder, eliminated every limit, broken every barrier, and lifted every lid! In the same way nothing can separate us from Their love (see Romans 8:38-39), nothing can separate, stop, or impede Their outpouring of love until it overflows in us! Our love clears the road, in the same way that our *"gift makes room"* for us (see Proverbs 18:16)

There's a special, inimitable strength and power that resides in *sameness* – power and resources to replicate. In the same way the Father, Son, and Holy Spirit (same Love) blessed and said, *"Be fruitful, multiply, and fill the earth, and subdue it [using all its vast resources in the service to God and man]; and have dominion..." "... [putting it under your power];"* to us through Adam & Eve; He has blessed us to *"increase and excel and overflow in love for one another and for all people."* In essence, our assignment is to subdue and have dominion by the *power of love*. (see Genesis 1:28 AMP included)

Overcome, Overflow, Outdo!

When we love this way – with an *increasing, excelling, overflowing* love, we are guaranteed to be given grace and strength. We are assured, *"So that He may strengthen and confirm and establish your hearts faultlessly pure and unblameable..."* (see 1 Thessalonians 3:13) By virtue of our union with The True Vine – because of our connection to Christ, we are approved or authorized for the

It's All We Can Eat!

assignment, and a current of strength flows, to empower us to continuously carry out our assignment.

One Greek word for confirm is bebaioo (beb-ah-yo-o). It means "to secure or stabilitate (establish)." Another Greek word is *episterizo* (ep-ee-stay-rid-zo). It means "to make stronger" or "support further." This is done by supporting, propping up, or upholding in a way that is fitting or suitable. Still, another Greek word is *kuroo* (koo-ro-o). It means "to make valid, reaffirm, assure." It's similar to the word *kurios* (koo-ree-os), which means "to ratify or make authoritative, or supreme in authority." Because we walk with Him and He works in and through us, we are already validated, as well as walking in authority and victory!

After reading those definitions, I am even more encouraged, confident, and feel more equipped to do what He has called me to do. I hope and pray that those definitions, as well as the following translations of 1 Thessalonians 3:13 bring more clarity and confidence to you, as well: *"May you be infused with strength and purity, filled with confidence in the presence of God our Father..."* (MSG) *"Then your hearts will be strengthened in holiness so that you may be flawless and pure before the face of our God and Father..."* (TPT) Because we are aware of, and rest in Him, *we wake up like this*!

When we embrace these truths – when we *"know the truth"* (see John 8:32) about Who He is, who we are, and what He has deposited in us; we are made free from the distraction of doubt, and *free, energized, and infused to flourish*! When we know that He's The One Who *validates* and *authenticates* us, doubt is dismantled and dismissed. We then walk in the liberty and limitless love that was released in us. This liberty and love exceeds any limitations anyone (including ourselves) attempts to put on them.

It's All We Can Eat!

     This is why we were encouraged, *"Never doubt God's mighty power to work in you and accomplish all this. He will achieve infinitely more than your greatest request, your most unbelievable dream, and exceed your wildest imagination! He will outdo them all, for <u>his miraculous power constantly energizes you</u>."* (Ephesians 3:20 TPT emphasis added)

It's "All We Can Eat!", Family. Let's Love Philanthropically!

Chapter 13
Come And Get It!

"For as these qualities are <u>yours and increasingly abound in you</u>, they will keep [you] from being idle or <u>unfruitful</u> unto the [<u>full personal</u>] knowledge of our Lord Jesus Christ (the Messiah, the Anointed One)."
(2 Peter 1:8)

In order live a lifestyle of *outdoing* ourselves, in terms of *showing honor, respect, and love to one another* (which is our proper response to His overflowing love for us); we must be or occupy the area where the outpouring and overflowing occurs. Whether you look at the townspeople who responded to the cry from the woman at the well, the disciples that united in the upper room on The Day of Pentecost, or those that gathered with Moses, when he caused water to rush out from within the rock; the common denominator is that a *decision* was made to dwell in the designated place where the delivery (or deliverance) would be dispensed. In other words, they were deliberate and devoted themselves to being at the *distribution center*!

In order for the infilling, infusing, or impartation, to be experienced; there must be an affirmative answer to the invitation. In other words, if we want to be *refreshed*, *renewed*, *refueled*, or *restored*; we have to R.S.V.P. Otherwise, we will remain weak and eventually fall to the ground, where we will wither, become worm-infested, and inevitably; *expire*!

The Invitation

"Come to Me, all you who labor and are heavy-laden and overburdened, and I will cause you to rest. [<u>I will ease and relieve and refresh your souls.</u>] ... you will find rest (relief and ease and <u>refreshment and recreation and blessed quiet</u>) for your souls." "all who are weary and heavily burdened [by religious rituals that provide no peace] ..." (see Matthew 11:28-30, AMP included, emphasis added) What we must realize is that the world is no longer looking for *religion*. In fact, *most of us*, as God's family of Believers, are done with religion, because we would much have a rich, rewarding, restful *relationship* with our Redeemer.

It's All We Can Eat!

Before I move on, I feel that it's important to point out The Passion Translation of this verse: *"Are you weary, carrying a heavy burden? Come to me. I will refresh your life, for I am your oasis. Simply join your life with mine. Learn my ways and you'll discover that I am gentle, humble, easy to please. You will find refreshment and rest in me. For all that I require of you will be pleasant and easy to bear."*

We all need rest, refreshment, refueling, and recovery from religion. Religion offers no relief, because it *requires us to do things in our own strength – by the flesh*. I've heard it said, that "Religion is man's effort to reach up to God, but *relationship* is God's effort to reach down to man." Man's idea of religion, and God's definition, are entirely different. "<u>Pure and undefiled</u> religion…" "<u>True spirituality</u> that is pure in the eyes of our Father is to <u>make a difference in the lives</u> of the orphans, and widows in their troubles, and to refuse to be corrupted by the world's values." (James 1:27 NKJV, TPT respectively, emphasis added)

God's brand of religion, like His brand of love, inspires us to *make a difference* – to have *relationship*. The Aramaic translates *"True spirituality"* as "True ministry." Also, orphans can be translated in Greek, as *orphanos* (or-fan-os), which can mean "comfortless" as well as "fatherless – being without a teacher, guide, or guardian." Making a difference and ministering comfort requires *the fruit of the Spirit* and *relationship*. Man's or the world's religion requires or provokes us to reach, but *relationship* provides us (and others) with *rest*, *peace*, *recreation*, and *refreshment* for our souls.

The Greek word for *"recreation"* is *anapsychi*. It also means "pleasure and relaxation." This is why He constantly calls to us to come to Him. In His Presence is where we come *"face-to-face"* with Him, and He presents or shows us *"the path of life."* It's also where there is *"fullness of joy"* and at His right hand, there are *"pleasures forevermore."* (see Psalms 16:11) I'm sure that this *"fullness of joy"* includes feasting on His faithfulness. Throughout the Bible, there's an abundance of references to His banquet table and feasts. Some that stick out to me, are Psalm 23:5, Psalm 107:9, Isaiah 25:6, Job 36:16, Ephesians 2:6, and Song of Solomon 2:4.

An Open Invitation

Sometimes, the table is set or stationed outside, in the open, where everyone has the opportunity to come unopposed and unobstructed, to drink and be satisfied. Isaiah prophesied, *"Wait and listen, everyone who is thirsty! Come to the waters; and he who has no money, come, buy and eat! Yes, come, buy [priceless, spiritual] wine and milk without money and without price [simply for the self-surrender that accepts the blessing] ...Hearken diligently to Me, and eat what is good, and let your soul delight itself in fatness [the profuseness of spiritual joy]."* (see Isiah 55:1-2)

Not only do we have open access to approach Him, unopposed and unobstructed – when we do so – we can also come *"to the waters"* without cost! Whether it's water, wine or milk – whatever we crave or hunger for, the cost of admission to consume *"what is good"* to our heart's content, without money; is our *"self-surrender"* or *acceptance of the invitation.*

Not only do we have open access to approach Him, and are authorized to freely consume to our heart's content; but wherever He is, He is *audible* – we can hear Him! He's not silent to His sheep who hear His voice (see John 10:27). We were taught, *"Now on the final and most important day of the Feast, Jesus stood, and He cried in a loud voice, If any man is thirsty let him come to Me and drink!"* (John 7:37) Wherever He strategically positions Himself, we are no longer lost, nor do we have to worry about the logistics. We can hear Him from wherever He is, and wherever we are. We can have life, and have it more abundantly (see John 10:10). Even at the Feast, you could say that He was *The Life of the party*!

As I alluded to above, He is accessible and audible. Wherever we're seated in His Presence *is premier or superior seating*! Here's an additional example of these powerful privileges: *"Wisdom cries aloud in the street, She raises her voice in the markets; She cries at the head of busy intersections [in the chief gathering places]; at the entrance of the city gates she speaks]: How long, O simple ones [open to evil], will you love being simple? And the scoffers delight in scoffing and the [self-confident] fools hate knowledge?"* (Proverbs 1:20-22) Wisdom is always looking for those wandering and wondering when life will or can better.

Wisdom is positioned, and pleads to the prideful, ignorant, pessimistic, uneducated, and evil. Much like music, Wisdom permeates the atmosphere – the song is sung – the symphony saturates the environment, inviting all to accept the invitation. Wisdom is *accommodating*. It doesn't matter what our economic, social, emotional, physical, educational, or financial status is – Wisdom will meet our needs!

The R.S.V.P.

I've known that R.S.V.P was a request for me to respond to an invitation sent to me. In short, it means "please reply." However, I didn't know the *official* definition. Please, don't judge me – I'm from the hood (LOL)! To those

It's All We Can Eat!

readers who also were place in a public school system, where we weren't taught this; R.S.V.P. is a French phrase – an initialism or acronym of *repondez, s'il vous plait*, meaning "reply, if you please." It is to confirm or notify the inviter of our intention to attend the event. In the same sense, the invitation for our refreshment, renewal, restoration – even our redemption requires our response or reply. There's power in our reply or response – in our R.S.V.P. to our Redeemer's invitations.

I stated earlier, that if we want to be *refreshed, renewed, refueled,* or *restored*; we have to R.S.V.P. I have my own acronym for R.S.V.P. It's Receive Strength Victory and Power. When we respond to The Lord, our Redeemer's invitation, the blessings or door prizes are *limitless*! Earlier, I wrote about the invitation of The Lord's Wisdom. It is written, *"Wisdom is so priceless that it exceeds the value of any jewel. Nothing you could wish for can equal her."* (Proverbs 8:11 TPT)

I mentioned above, that being *"comfortless"* can mean being "without a teacher, guide, or guardian." When we accept the invitation – when we R.S.V.P. we receive our Teacher, Guide and Guardian. He is our Teacher and advises us, *"Take My yoke upon you and learn of Me...For My yoke is wholesome (useful, good...comfortable, gracious, and pleasant..." "I will refresh your life, for I am your oasis. Simply join your life with mine. Learn my ways and you'll discover that I'm gentle, humble, easy to please...For all that I require of you will be pleasant and easy to bear."* (see Matthew 11:28-30, TPT included)

As our Teacher, He gives us *hands-on* training. He knows that the process isn't easy, so He invites us to take His yoke upon us, and learn of and from Him. In other words,

He wants us to walk beside Him, *step-by-step*, receiving instruction and refreshment simultaneously. He has also taught us that He would never leave us *"comfortless"* or without a *Comforter*. This is why He promised, *"And I will ask the Father, and He will give you another Comforter (Counselor, Helper, Intercessor, Advocate, Strengthener, and Standby), that He may remain with you forever—"* (John 14:16).

The Greek word used for *"Comforter"* is *parakletos* (par-ak-lay-tos). It means "called to one's aid." Jesus was speaking of The Holy Spirit, the One who walks alongside of us, to aid and assist us. Another word is *paraclete*. It's a legal term that means "a *legal advocate* who makes the right judgment-*call* because they are *close* enough to the situation." Because The Holy Spirit is close enough to us (alongside and inside us), and close enough to God (He Is God), He can make the right judgement calls – accurate assessments, and give us excellent advice or correct or incorruptible counsel. *"...He will teach you all things. And He will cause you to recall (will remind you of, bring to your remembrance) everything I have told you."* (see John 14:26)

We don't have a substitute teacher – we have a Master Teacher, Guardian, and a Guidance Counselor. *"But when He, the Spirit of Truth (the Truth-giving Spirit) comes, He will guide you into all the Truth (the whole, full Truth) ..."* (John 16:13) Even through the work of the Holy Spirit, we learn of the Lord, as we remain *yoked* to Him. This is why we are instructed, *"If we live by the [Holy] Spirit, let us also walk by the Spirit. [If by the Holy Spirit we have our life in God, let us go forward walking in line, our conduct controlled by the Spirit."* (Galatians 5:25)

Long before mankind manufactured the technology, The Lord had already provided a spiritual GPS (Godly Positioning System). John 16:13, in part, reads, *"But when the Friend comes, the Spirit of Truth, <u>he will take you by the hand and guide you</u> into all the truth there is." "...he will unveil the reality of every <u>truth within you</u>."* (MSG, TPT, emphasis added) Early on, in my Christian walk, I learned *what a Friend we have in Jesus*. Unfortunately, it took decades for me to learn how much of a Friend the Holy Spirit Is.

God is always willing to guide us. He doesn't want His children misguided or unguarded. God said, *"I will stay close to you, instructing and <u>guiding you along the pathway</u> for your life. I will advise you along the way and lead you forth <u>with my eyes as your guide</u>."* It's a matter of trusting Him with all of our heart, instead of our own logic, or other people's advice or opinions. *"With all your heart <u>rely on him to guide you</u>, <u>and he will lead you in every decision you make</u>. Become intimate with him in whatever you do, and <u>he will lead you wherever you go</u>."* (see Psalm 32:8, Proverbs 3:5-6 TPT emphasis added)

The Lord not only guides and positions us, but He also guards and protects us. He shows up as Guardian because He is our Shepherd. He said, *"I am the Good Shepherd. The Good Shepherd risks and lays down His [own] life for the sheep." "And I give them eternal life, and they shall never lose it or perish throughout the ages. [To all eternity they shall never by any means be destroyed.] And no one is able to snatch them out of My hand. My Father, Who has given them to me, is greater and mightier than all [else]; and no one is able to snatch [them] out of the Father's hand. I and the Father are One."* (John 10:11, 28-30)

It's All We Can Eat!

And the Psalmist David declared, *"The Lord is my Shepherd [to feed, guide, and shield me], I shall not lack. He makes me lie down in [fresh, tender] green pastures; He leads me beside the still and restful waters. He refreshes and restores my life (my self); ...Yes, though I walk through the [deep, sunless] valley of the shadow of death, I will fear or dread no evil, for You are with me; Your rod [to protect] and Your staff [to guide], they comfort me...Surely or only goodness, mercy, and unfailing love shall follow me all the days of my life..."* (see Psalm 23) All of this; education, guidance, protection, and so much more, is available, as we accept His invitation.

When we R.S.V.P., we reserve our place to receive all of the advocacy, comfort, help, counsel, intercession, instruction, and strength that we need; all on a daily, whenever necessary, for as long as necessary, as much as necessary basis. In other words, when we R.S.V.P. – when we reply with our belief, we receive recurring *"rivers"* of relief and refreshment beyond our imagination, and they *emanate or issue from inside of us*. It couldn't be any closer or more convenient than that! The best part about it, is that some of the needs are met, before we even know that they are a need! God said, *"And it shall be that before they call I will answer; and while they are yet speaking I will hear."* (Isaiah 65:24)

At the risk of sounding like an informercial, I'm going to insert this next sentence: BUT WAIT, *THERE'S MORE!!!* When we R.S.V.P., we are automatically registered to continually receive refreshment from The River of Life, for the *rest* of our lives! When we speak to our Rock and River of Life, we're sending Him our R.S.V.P. When we R.S.V.P., we're saying to Him that we believe in Him, we're cleaving to Him, we trust Him, we're clinging to Him, and we're relying on Him, for rest, relief, relaxation, refreshment, and restoration. We're relaying to or letting Him that we love, live in, and rely on Him.

What a blessing this is, but more than the blessings, we must make sure that we *believe in Him*! Our River and Rock promised us, *"He who believes in Me [who cleaves to and trusts in and relies on Me] as the Scripture has said, From his innermost being shall flow [continuously] springs and rivers of living water." "...Believe in me so that rivers of living water will burst within you, flowing from your innermost being..." "...Rivers of living water will brim and spill out of the depths of anyone who believes in me this way..."* (see John 7:37-38 TPT, MSG included, emphasis added)

In the same way that water rushed from the rock to refresh the Israelites in the wilderness; the Lord, our Rock, will *refresh* us! However, instead of striking like Moses did, we must *speak* to the Rock. When I researched this, I discovered something. It reads, *"...assemble the congregation and speak to the rock in front of them, so that it will pour out its water." "And the water poured out abundantly, and the congregation and their livestock drank [fresh water]."* (see Numbers 20:8-11 AMP emphasis added)

The Hebrew word used for *"water"* is *mayim* (mah-yim). It can mean "waters" and "flood." Hebrew word used for *"pour out"* is *nathan* (naw-than). It can mean "to deliver, to distribute, to give, to be given, generously give" and my favorite, "gift." What I saw and heard was that sometimes, when we R.S.V.P. – when we speak to The Rock, we're not just doing so for ourselves, but also for those who are with us – those who God has *assigned* to us. Both we, and they

It's All We Can Eat!

receive a *gift*, much like a door prize is received, when we attend some events.

When we R.S.V.P. – when we speak to The Rock in front of them, *living water* not only flows from Him, but also, out of our bellies – out of our depths, and it then flows to them, and *floods* their lives, so that they can be revived and refreshed. In other words, He is not only our Rock, but He's also or River and *Gift*! So, when we reply or R.S.V.P. to Him – even *"in front of them"* we not only receive the *Gift*, but we also *deliver* or *distribute the Gift* to them! Therefore, we must not remain silent. There are so many who need *"living rivers"* and *encouragement* to flood or overflow into their lives, homes, timelines, news feeds, etc.

As we are refreshed and encouraged, we are then, empowered and equipped to encourage, empower, and equip others. However, in order for this to happen, we've got to be willing to *obey* our thirst. Belief begins with obedience. Like David, we must declare or speak to The Rock, *"My deep need calls out to the deep kindness of your love."* (see Psalm 42:7 TPT) In response, *"rivers of living water"* rush through us, and out to others. We can then, say to ourselves and to them, *"Look at how much encouragement you have found <u>in your relationship with the Anointed One</u>! You are <u>filled to overflowing with his comforting love</u>. You have experienced <u>a deepening friendship</u> with the Holy Spirit and have felt his <u>tender affection and mercy</u>."* (Philippians 2:1 TPT emphasis added)

What's On The Menu? Soul Food!

When we refuse to reply or respond to the invitation to be present, we not only relinquish our right or privilege to free food – we also have to resort to eating at a different restaurant – one which may not serve rich, robust entrees and delicacies, as those that were available and included with the *invitation* that was declined. However, this wouldn't be the first time in history that this has happened. Hosea wrote, *"For they shall eat and not have enough…"* (4:10a) Also, Haggai heralded, *"You have sown much, but you have reaped little; you eat, but you do not have enough; you drink, but you do not have your fill…"* (see 1:6)

A similar judgement was meted out in Micah, where it is written, *"You shall eat but not be satisfied, and your emptiness and hunger shall remain in you…You shall sow but not reap; you shall tread olives but not anoint yourselves with oil, and [you shall extract juice from] the grapes but not drink the wine."* (see 6:14-15) The message is crystal clear: they ate and drank, but were *not* merry! They had food, but *not* fulfillment! They had something to sip on, but *not* satisfaction!

Whenever we're finished feasting in the natural – at the conclusion of our consumption, we still have to come to grips with the fact that in our steps to be satisfied; our souls are still hungry and thirsty, because there's only One Who can truly satisfy our hunger and thoroughly quench that thirst! As I expressed earlier, we've got to be willing to obey our thirst, because both, our belief and refreshment begin with our obedience. What's needed is a daily desire, identical to the Psalmist David and sons of Korah, when they sang, *"As the deer pants [longingly] for the water brooks, So my soul pants [longingly] for You, O God. My soul (my life, my inner self) thirsts for God, for the living God. When will I come and see the face of God?"* (Psalm 42:1-2 AMP)

When we obey or cooperate with our thirst, and constantly *"come and see the face of God"*, we find refreshment, and *"He brings gifts into our lives, much the same way that fruit appears in an orchard..."* (Galatians 5:22 MSG). We will then, hear the whisper of The Holy Spirit, echoing the words of approval from our Heavenly Father. We will also realize our responsibility as Believers, as we are reminded of the lessons, examples, and the legacy Lord left us to look at:

"And consider the example that Jesus, the Anointed One, has set before us. <u>Let his mindset become your motivation</u>...<u>he emptied himself of his outward glory by reducing himself</u>...<u>He humbled himself</u> and became vulnerable...choosing to be revealed as a man and was <u>obedient</u>...<u>Because of that obedience</u>, <u>God exalted him and multiplied his greatness</u>!" (see Philippians 2:5-11 TPT emphasis added)

Our food must be to do the will of The Father (see John 4:34). No other meal is more nourishing. Nothing else can be served to us or set before us, that satisfies our souls or multiplies our strength or greatness. When we respond in righteousness and obedience, and the recipe is revealed to us, we will discover that the main ingredient is love. Then we will sing like the Psalmist, *"My soul [my life, my very self] is satisfied..." "...for the anointing of your presence satisfies me like nothing else. You are such a rich banquet of pleasure to my soul."* (Psalm 63:5 AMP, TPT) *"For He satisfies the longing soul and fills the hungry soul with goodness"* (Psalm 107:9)

It's "All We Can Eat!", Family. Let's Love Like The Lord!

Chapter 14
Go Get It!

"Since these virtues are <u>already planted deep within</u>, and <u>you possess them in abundant supply</u>, they will keep you from being inactive or fruitless in your pursuit of knowing Jesus Christ more intimately."
(2 Peter 1:8 TPT)

It's All We Can Eat!

As a child, I wasn't a big fan of watching the westerns on TV. However, the one thing that sticks out to me, it is at the supper time scenes, when someone would ring the bell or triangle, to signal that supper (lunch or dinner) was ready. Sometimes, the bell was a steel triangle, and the person ringing it would yell out, "Commme annn' gettt ittt!" I vaguely recall Granny, from the sitcom *The Beverly Hillbillies* doing this.

Get The Door!

Still today, a bell or triangle is ringing for us to *come and get it*. However, the triangle ringing is, The Holy Trinity (Father, Son, Holy Spirit). In the spirit realm, supper is always available to us. In other words, there's a seat and the table is always set for us in *"heavenly places"* (see Ephesians 2:6). As an eight-year-old, in the children's ward of Crozer-Chester Medical Center, I was seated and had my first spiritual supper, after accepting a simple invitation. A Nun read us a Bible Story, sang us a song, as she played her acoustic guitar, and then read us this Bible verse: *"Behold, I stand at the door, and knock: if any man hear my voice, and open the door, I will come in to him, and will sup with him, and he with me."* (Revelation 3:20 KJV)

After she explained that the Lord was standing at the door my heart and knocking, my eight-year-old soul heard the whisper of The Holy Spirit, and opened the door to my heart, and let Him in. At that time, I didn't fully understand or realize all of the ramifications and implications of the invitation. However, as I wrote this chapter, I decided to do a short study.

Here's the verse from a few of my favorite translations: *"Behold, I stand at the door [of the church] and*

It's All We Can Eat!

continually knock. If anyone hears My voice and opens the door, I will come in and eat with him (restore him), and he with Me." (AMP) *"...if anyone hears and listens to and heeds My voice..."* (AMPC) *"Look at me. I stand at the door. I knock. If you hear me call and open the door, I'll come right in and sit down to supper with you."* (MSG) *"...If your heart is open to hear my voice and you open the door within, I will come in to you and feast with you, and you will feast with me."* (TPT emphasis added)

The Greek word for *"sup"* is *deipneo* (dipe-neh-o). It means "to eat, dine." of course, that comes as no surprise, right? I mean, it's not exactly "Breaking News", right? However, in my studies, I did discover something surprising. I noticed a reference to 1 Corinthians 11:25, which details the Lord's Last Supper with His disciples. The reference noted, "I will make him to share in my most intimate and blissful contact." It reminded me of a conversation I had years ago with someone, while selling my t-shirts at a mall. She told me that having supper with someone was one of the most intimate acts performed. If I correctly recall, she was referring to customs and culture during the time Christ was teaching His disciples.

Today, in order for us to experience such *intimacy* with Him, we must get the door. In other words, we must open the door of our heart to *The Door* of our salvation and restoration. He promised, *"I am the Door; anyone who enters in through Me will be saved (will live). He will come in and he will go out [freely], and will find pasture." "...To enter through me is to experience life, freedom, and satisfaction."* (John 10:9, TPT included, emphasis added)

It's interesting to me, that the Amplified version of Revelation 3:20 parenthetically uses the phrase *"restore*

It's All We Can Eat!

him", as it pertains to the Lord eating with those who open their door to Him. It makes sense, since we are promised that He will restore our souls when we come to Him (see Psalm 23:5, Matthew 11:28). Our opening or *getting* the door and letting Him in is reminiscent of a custom during that time in His culture. It was an ancient Jewish wedding invitation, in which the bridegroom and father would arrive at the door of the house of the bride to be. He would have with him, the betrothal cup of wine and the bride-price. They would stand outside and knock. If she fully opened the door, she was acknowledging that she was accepting the invitation to be his bride.

In the same way, over 2,000 years later, He, the Door or Bridegroom, and our Heavenly Father still stand at our door, with *the cup containing everything we need* for healing, restoration, fellowship; knocking and waiting for us to answer and accept His invitation to *feast with Him forever*! Also interesting is what seems to be a role or responsibility reversal. We are commanded, *"Keep on asking and it will be given you; keep on seeking and you will find; <u>keep on knocking [reverently] and [the door] will be opened to you.</u>"* (Matthew 7:7 emphasis added)

However, in Revelation 3:20, it's our Redeemer, Who *seeks, asks, and knocks*! Here's the blessing for those who *"hears and listens to and heeds"* His voice, opens their door, and allows *The Door* to enter: *"Behold, I'm standing at the door, knocking. <u>If your heart is open to hear</u> my voice and you <u>open the door within</u>, I will come in to you and feast with you, and <u>you will feast with me</u>. And the to <u>the one who conquers</u> I will give the privilege of <u>sitting with me on my throne</u>, just as I conquered and sat down with my Father on *his throne."* (Revelation 3:20-21 TPT emphasis added) We get *all of this*, when we get *The Door*!

Your Order Was Delivered!

I'm an Amazon Prime Member. Other than the USPS (United States Postal Service), the Amazon delivery person comes to my door more than anyone else. Whether I am home, or away, packages are delivered, and I receive a notification on my cell phone stating "Your package was delivered." If I'm home, all I to do is go to the door and get my package. Oh, how convenient!

I want to remind you (and me) that we have some packages. We have orders that were delivered to us, and they're waiting for us to get them. No; we didn't order them, and the packages aren't on our porch or at our doorstep. They were *ordered* by our Heavenly Father and delivered to us before our birth. These packages were placed, or deposited deep *within us*. However, they are ineffective in that environment. It's like fruit or a tree, in its seed form, deep within the soil. No one can feed from them, nor do the seed or fruit fulfill their purpose; if they remain unearthed, undeveloped, unknown, and unused.

That's because being or remaining unearthed, undeveloped, unknown, and unused; is *unfruitful*. This is not the will of our Heavenly Father for our lives. On the contrary, we were commanded to *"be fruitful and multiply"* and to keep ourselves *"from being idle or unfruitful."* (see Genesis 1:28, 2 Peter 1:8) Therefore, being fruitless or unfruitful is not an option, nor negotiable. It's not only inexcusable and unacceptable, but it's also impossible to be intimately connected to Christ, and *the fruit of the Spirit* not produce fruit or have a harvest from our lives.

It's All We Can Eat!

Act Like You Know!

During my junior high and high school years, I was exposed to quite a bit of colloquialisms. It seemed as if slang terminology was some people's primary language or second nature! One phrase that was pretty prominent among my peers was, "You better *act like you know*!" It was a sarcastic reaction said to someone who said or did something that was not approved or appreciated by the recipient of the statement or deed. Perhaps, this phrase was an abbreviation of our parents' warning to us; "You better *act like you know better*, or else!" No matter what the origin, if we knew what was best for us, we heeded the warning – whether it was from our parents or our peers!

Long before that colloquialism, our Heavenly Father had commanded that we act like we knew. Although it was imperative to Him that we know what He had implanted in us, more importantly, He wanted us to know *Who* was embedded in, equipping, and empowering us! As I previously stated, we *already* have what we need to be *fruitful*. Our fertility is unquestionable, and as you will see in a few seconds, it's also *irrefutable*! We are assured, *"For as these qualities are yours…" "Since these virtues are already planted deep within."* (see 2 Peter 1:8, TPT included, emphasis added) Plain and simple, *we already possess* the power!

In fact, one of the Greek words used for *"possess"* is *huparchonta* (hoop-ar-khon-tah), which means "in hand, i.e., property – goods, substance." It's a variation of the word *huparxis* (hoop-arx-is), which means "existency or proprietorship, i.e. wealth." In other words, these qualities or virtues – this property or wealth – these possessions are inextricably implanted within us! There's a certain assurance or confidence that comes with knowing we are owners of property or possessors of wealth. Therefore, we must *act like we know* what God has given us, and carry out the actions required to accomplish the assignments He has given us, using vast wealth and virtues He has already implanted within us!

Value Virtue!

As I alluded to in an earlier chapter, as our faithfulness is being nourished and enlarged, *we develop* our *"virtue"*, which was already attached or *"closely joined"* to our growing faith. As we endeavor to, and acquire an *ever-increasing faith*, it will develop in us an *ever-increasing* virtue. As stated earlier, the Greek word for *"virtue"* is *arete* (ar-et-ay). It means "moral excellence which is displayed to enrich life." It also means "goodness, gracious act, uprightness."

Another Greek word for *"virtue"*, as used in Luke 8:46, is *dunamis* (doo-nam-is). It means "ability, abundance, power, strength, mighty (wonderful) work. As it pertains to this chapter, it also means "the power and influence which belong to riches and wealth", as well as "inherent power" – power *residing* in a person, *which they exert or put forth*. A similar spelling for this Greek word is *dynamis*. For the Believer, means "power to achieve by applying the Lord's inherent abilities." In other words, power through God's ability. The virtue or power that God deposited in us wasn't meant to lie dormant. These virtues were *invested* – this power was implanted in us, in order for us to put forth or *exert it to produce an abundant harvest*!

This endowment of power or quality of life is given to us *to be productive and fruitful* and is intrinsic to our intimate relationship with Christ. This is why He said, "...*Whoever lives in Me and I in him bears much (abundant) fruit*..." "*So you must remain in life-union with me, for I remain in life-union with you.*" "*...your life will be fruitless unless you live your life intimately joined to mine...*" "*...As you live in union with me as your source, fruitfulness will stream from within you – but when you live separated from me you are powerless.*" (see John 15:4-5 TPT included, emphasis added)

It is our *"life-union"* with The True Vine, which serves as the vessel or venue, through which virtue is implanted and vibrates within us. Virtue was invested or embedded in us *to enrich our lives,* as well as to enrich the lives of *others*. Our virtue is neither to draw attention to ourselves, nor add value to us, while devaluing others. Instead, it is intended to add value to, and show others, *views of God's glory and versions of His love*, as well as invite them into a *"life-union"* with Him.

It's through the *"exercising"* and developing of our virtue, that we *"[develop] knowledge (intelligence)"*, which we are invited to acquire. This invitation to invest in gaining intelligence – the gift of gaining *"the [full, personal] knowledge of Him"* is initiated or inspired by God Himself. More specifically, He "*called us by and to His own glory and excellence (virtue).*" (2 Peter 1:3)   His virtue and glory are so great, and He values us so much, that His excellence *invites* us to know Him *more intimately*!

I'm going to hit the rewind button, and go back for a moment. *"For as these qualities are yours..."* "*Since these virtues are already planted deep within, and you possess them...*" When the Apostle Peter penned this, he wasn't just pointing out a fact, he was providing us with *truth*. He was also presenting us with a precious promise. In fact, the word *"within"* provides a vital key to validating this promise. The Greek word used for *"within"* is *huparcho* (hoop-ar-kho). It means "to begin under (quietly), to be ready or at hand." A variation is *hyparcho*, which means "to begin below" (or "within," like a plant growing beneath the ground). Its usage is "I am, begin, exist, am in possession." As stated above, it is a variation of the Greek word *huparxis* (hoop-arx-is), which means "existency or proprietorship, i.e., property, wealth, substance." Basically, it means "to already have (be in possession of); what pre-exists." Say to yourself, out loud, "I got it!"

In other words, we were *prepackaged*! Prior to our birth, and before we heard the call, we had a *preexisting condition*. Before we entered or invaded Earth's environment, we were embedded with virtues. The Apostle Paul praised and pronounced blessings on *"...the God and Father of our Lord Jesus Christ (the Messiah) Who has <u>blessed us in Christ with every spiritual (given by the Holy Spirit) blessing</u> in the heavenly realm! Even as [in His love] He chose us [actually picked us out for Himself as His own] in Christ before the foundation of the world, that we should be holy (consecrated and set apart for Him) and blameless in His sight, even above reproach, before Him in love."* (see Ephesians 1:3-4 emphasis added)

This takes being "blessed to be a blessing" to another level or greater heights (no pun intended). Because our Heavenly Father loves us, He picked us to be His, sending us the Holy Spirit, Who lives *in* us, because of Christ, Who is *in* God, Who also lives *in* us! You can call it a "package deal", or "an inside job." However, I choose to call it *love*!

It's All We Can Eat!

The Passion Translation reads, *"Every spiritual blessing in the heavenly realm has <u>already been lavished upon us as a love gift</u> from our wonderful heavenly Father, the Father of our Lord Jesus – all because He sees us <u>wrapped into Christ</u>..."* (emphasis added) The phrase *"wrapped into Christ"* reminded me of chapter 2, where I referenced Colossians 3:14: *"And above all these [put on] love and enfold yourselves with the bond of perfectness [which binds everything together completely in ideal harmony]."* I was also reminded of a note I saw during my devotional reading, the day before I wrote this section of this chapter.

In The Passion Translation, John 12:32 reads, *"And I will do this when I am lifted up off the ground and when I draw the hearts of people <u>to gather them to me</u>."* (emphasis added) According to my commentary notes, this verse could be translated "I will draw all things to myself." Or "I will bundle everyone / everything next to me." This really blessed me, and confirmed what I thought, concerning the consistency and intention of our Heavenly Father, as displayed in these three verses. It's so amazing to know that we have been drawn to Christ, and that being bundled or *wrapped into* Him, includes *already having every spiritual blessing lavished upon us as a love gift*!

Alive And Active!

"For as these qualities are <u>yours and increasingly abound in you</u>, they will keep [you] from being idle or <u>unfruitful</u> unto the [full personal] knowledge of our Lord Jesus Christ (the Messiah, the Anointed One)."
(2 Peter 1:8)

It's All We Can Eat!

There are three things that we are assured of are:

> ➢ *"For the Word that God speaks is <u>alive and full of power [making it active, operative, energizing, and effective]</u>; it is sharper than any two-edged sword..."* (Hebrews 4:12 emphasis added)

> ➢ *"...for it is God Who is all the while <u>effectually at work in you</u> [energizing and creating in you the power and desire] ..."* (Philippians 2:13 emphasis added)

> ➢ *"Now to Him Who, by (in consequence of) the <u>[action of His] power that is at work within us</u>, is able to [carry out His purpose and] do super abundantly, far over and above all that we [dare] ask or think..."* (Ephesians 3:20 emphasis added)

He Who began a *"good work"* in us is faithful to perform, finish, or perfect it (see Philippians 1:6); because He not only authorized it, but He is also *actively involved* and abides in us, along with the good work! Since this is the case, where's the disconnect? I had to ask myself, "Why isn't my barn bursting with abundance? Why doesn't my distribution center cater to more people in need of the fruit of the Spirit?" I believe I discovered why my ability to produce and distribute is diminished, inactive, or dormant. I believe it's because at times, I'm not always in *agreement* with God.

As I was reading various versions of Hebrews 4:12, I discovered something in The Passion Translation. It reads,

It's All We Can Eat!

"For we have the living Word of God, which is full of energy, like a two-mouthed sword..." The term *"two-mouthed"* means, "God speaks His word, then we, in agreement, also speak His word and it becomes a "two-mouthed sword." This reminds me of what I wrote in chapter 3: *"Above all, constantly echo God's intense love..."* (see 1 Peter 4:8 TPT)

Since God so loved us, that He spoke life into us, *began a good work in* us, and gave us *everything that pertains to life and godliness – that we might have life more abundantly*; our response should be to not only *agree* with Him, but to also *echo* how He has loved us, as well as echo and execute what He commanded us to do: *bear abundant fruit*!

Our agreeing with God is in essence, us participating – playing our part, or performing our portion of the *partnership* or agreement. Unless and until we agree with God, His power in us, to produce abundant harvests will remain an *inactive ingredient*. However, when we agree with Him, and *echo* what He is saying, we *activate* His power in us! This also assists us in accepting the reality that we *already* possess the power to produce. It just has to be *ignited* or activated!

Order In The Court

Now, I'm not an Attorney, nor have I studied law. However, if I were, I would attempt to set a precedent by submitting 2 Peter 1:8 as evidence as to why we not only have the right, but we also have a *responsibility* to bear abundant harvests. I would layout my argument concerning our authority and ability, using various versions of that verse, in the following manner:

To support my case, in my opening statement, I would cite 2 Peter 1:8 from the Expanded Bible version which reads, *"Because you have these blessings…"* I would follow up by adding, *"But the fruit produced by the Holy Spirit within you…"* (found in Galatians 5:22 TPT) to establish that we are *already blessed* by God. We are blessed with blessings, and we're also blessed *to be* blessings! Ephesians 1:3 explains that He *"has blessed us in Christ with every spiritual (given by the Holy Spirit) blessing in the heavenly realm!"* Every good and perfect gift comes from above, from our Heavenly Father (see James 1:17). Therefore, they will not fade or falter, nor will they be found faulty.

Once I established that we are blessed by God and I have identified the intrinsic value and immeasurable power we possess, I would indicate God's expectation – what we are instructed to do with these blessings. It's a forgone conclusion that we have a full complement or total possession of the blessings. However, it might be important to insert the statement, *"These are the qualities you need…"* (GNT) We must know that what we were blessed to possess is a *necessity*! We also need to know the purpose of what we possess. The late, illustrious Dr. Myles Munroe taught me, "When purpose is not known, abuse is inevitable."

I would then proceed by pointing out the certainty of our possessions, and our proper response to what we have received. Some versions begin, *"For as these qualities are yours…"* (AMP), *"For if you possess these qualities…"* (NIV), *"For if you possess these traits…"* (Voice) I believe that understanding our stewardship, ownership, or possession produces confidence and boosts our self-esteem; especially as we have an accurate estimation or have properly appraised – if we have accurately assessed what we possess and are blessed with.

However, possession, ownership, and self-esteem, altogether are still insufficient, regarding fruit production or reaping a harvest. In other words, an accurate estimation is not enough – there must be *intentional activation*! A more appropriate term is *constant cultivation*. Therefore, we have such stipulations as: *"and increasingly abound in you", "in increasing measure", "If you keep growing in this way", "and multiply them", "if you have them in abundance", "The more you grow like this", "For as these qualities are yours and are increasing [in you as you grow toward spiritual maturity]"*

Unless we commit ourselves to the intentional activation and *constant cultivation* of what we already possess, what we experience will be *stagnation*. Whatever amount we produce will be *inappropriate*. In other words it will be insufficient, in proportion to what is necessary to meet the needs of the people, and the expectation of our Heavenly Father. What's been divinely deposited in us is supposed to flow *through* us – not just *to* us! We must view ourselves as vessels of living water. Just as a river reaches throughout a region, refreshing the root systems of the vegetation surrounding it, we must be equally as far-reaching and refreshing to people. This is part of what it means to be *alive and active*.

By doing so, instead of being stagnant, we prevent ourselves from being impotent or powerless. In other words, when we have a proclivity for proactivity and productivity, it precludes us from unproductivity and infertility! In fact, the above Bible verse says that our activity and productivity prevent us from being *"ineffective and unproductive"*, *"useless"* and by implication, *meaningless*!

On the contrary, we become or are made *"useful and meaningful."* It will also illustrate or *"show that what you know about our Lord Jesus Christ..."* – there will be a revelation *"in regard to the true knowledge and greater understanding of our Lord Jesus Christ."* This is why it is imperative that we live our lives in a state of *intentional activation* or *constant cultivation*. Otherwise, we may be viewed as *"wicked, and lazy, and idle"* like the servant in Matthew 25:26.

The Love Ladder

Prior to this precedence of proactivity and productivity, there is a passage of Scripture right before it, that could prove to bring clarity. In verses five through seven we are given a formula for being fruitful, which has as the foundational ingredient, *faith*. It is on this foundation or basis of faith, that we must *add to* or build upon with the other virtues.

In an earlier chapter, I explained that one of my Bibles describes the section of 2 Peter 1:5-11 as *Faith's Ladder of Virtue*. To me, this means that in the same way that it takes more than one rung or step for a ladder to be considered a ladder, and elevate you to the next level; it takes more than one step, characteristic, or virtue being added to our faith for it to constitute being a *ladder of faith*. Furthermore, it takes more than one act or characteristic to be added, in order to be considered a *ladder of love*!

Even as we add one virtue to the other, the previous virtue must remain active. We must remember that this is an *addition* process, not a subtraction or substitution process.

They must all work together, just like our body parts! Concerning the Body of Christ, it is explained in Ephesians 4:16, *"For his "body" has been formed in his image and is <u>closely joined together and constantly connected as one</u>. And every member has been given divine gifts to <u>contribute to the growth of all</u>; and as these gifts operate effectively throughout the whole body, we are built up and made perfect in love."* (TPT emphasis added) The Amplified reads, *"...when each part is working properly, causes the body to grow and mature, building itself up in [unselfish] love."*

During my studies, I discovered that it is possible to view the 2 Peter 1:5-11 passage as "an unfolding of faith" according to The Passion Translation footnotes. This is what I call a "Love Ladder." It reads, "Out of your faith will emerge goodness, and out of goodness will emerge understanding (of God), and out of understanding (of God) will emerge inner strength (self-control), and out of inner strength will emerge patient endurance, and out of patient endurance will emerge godliness, and out of godliness will emerge mercy toward your brothers and sisters, and out mercy will emerge love." It almost appears as if love emerges only *after* all other virtues have been engaged.

I also discovered that it is also possible to view this passage as a mathematical equation. The notes continued, "Faith + goodness = understanding. Goodness + understanding = inner strength. Understanding + inner strength = patience. Inner strength + patience = godliness. Patience + godliness = mercy. And godliness + mercy = love." This really blessed me, by presenting me with a better or the proper perspective!

Although I've already written it a few times, I feel that it's necessary to reiterate Apostle Peter's revelation in 2

Peter 1:8. It reads, *"For as these qualities <u>are yours and increasingly abound in you</u>, they will keep [you] from being idle or unfruitful unto the [full personal] knowledge of our Lord Jesus Christ (the Messiah, the Anointed One)."* The TPT reads, *"Since these virtues are <u>already planted deep within</u>, and <u>you possess them in abundant supply</u>..."* (emphasis added) The footnotes include "Or 'abounding' (repeatedly being more than enough)."

The alternate Arabic Translation uses the word "abounding" which means "repeatedly being more than enough." Our Heavenly Father, El Shaddai is not only The God Who is More Than Enough, He also makes sure that we have more than enough! We have more than enough to expand, increase, become fruitful, and flourish, as we express His love! In other words, our response to His love for us, is making sure that we are more than enough for those who are in need of the love that we possess.

However, to be fruitful and flourish, these virtues and expressions must be activated by our faith. Therefore, we must devote ourselves to *"lavishly supplementing"* our faith. Our primary perception must be our *partnership*. The Greek word used for participate, in verse four is *koinonos*. Some of its meanings are, "to participate as a partner" and to be a companion with." Our Heavenly has already done His part, or participated by deeply implanting the virtues in us. So, we must do our part – we must participate or *partner* with Him, by diligently implementing what He has deeply implanted in us, to induce growth and produce fruit.

Until we respond in obedience, by claiming, embracing, and cultivating the precious promises, what's contained in them – their power won't be released. That's because our faith releases or unleashes the unlimited power of the Word of God. However, this isn't a passive process or procedure. We must proceed or exercise our faith by having *added our intense effort*! When we add our intense effort, we will increase in our knowledge of Christ. When we increase in our knowledge of Christ, we're able or capable of doing *exploits*. In fact, we will *excel* in our exploits!

Daniel 11:32 reads, *"...but the people who [are spiritually mature and] know their God will display strength and take action [to resist]."* (AMP) *"...shall prove themselves strong and shall stand firm and do exploits [for God]."* (AMPC) *"...but the people who know their God shall be strong, and carry out great exploits."* (KJV) The Hebrew word used for *"exploits"* is *asah* (aw-saw). Besides meaning "do, make", some other meanings are "accomplish much, achieve, advance, execute, fulfill, indeed perform, produce" and "thoroughly deal." Other forms of the word can mean "God has made" and "made by God." It is through our knowledge of Christ, that we that discover who we are – who God has made. Once we discover that we're *made by God* we are activated or enabled to achieve or do great exploits for Him.

If you've been a Believer for a few years, you've probably heard, or maybe even said to yourself, "It's a *faith* walk!" As I typed that, the thought that occurred to me is that there's a difference between a step and a *walk*. A step is defined as "a movement made by lifting the foot and setting it down again in a new position, accompanied by a shifting of the weight of the body in the direction of the new position, as in walking, running, or dancing." A walk is defined as "advance by steps; to advance or travel on foot at a moderate speed or pace; proceed by steps; move by advancing the feet alternately." Unless we make the distinction between a step and a walk, we will be delayed, if not also detoured, and denied from reaching our destination or destiny.

As you can see, we can take a step, without walking. However, we cannot take a walk without taking multiple steps. As the *"just"* and the *"righteous"*, we are called and required to walk and live by faith (see Romans 1:17, Galatians 3:11). I believe both verses can be traced back to Habakkuk 2:4, which reads, *"Look at the proud; his soul is not straight or right within him, but the [rigidly] just and the [uncompromisingly] righteous man shall live by his faith and in his faithfulness."* Reading this, caused me to ask the questions, "Could it be that my soul wasn't right, and my success was stagnated or prevented because of pride? Is the reason that I wasn't *"straight"* because I wasn't not living a just and righteous life?"

I was prompted to read a related Scripture passage. Hebrews 10:38 reads, *"But the just shall live by faith [My righteous servant shall live by his conviction respecting man's relationship to God and divine things, and holy fervor born of faith and conjoined with it]; and if he draws back and shrinks in fear, My soul has no delight or pleasure in him."* The Passion Translation reads, *"And he also says, "My righteous ones will live from my faith. But if fear holds them back, my soul is not content with them!"*

Once again, after reading this, I was left wondering, "Am I just, while on my journey – am I living by His commands and based on my convictions, born of faith? Am I living from and *walking – taking steps* by His faith, or do I draw or shrink back, because of my fears?" This is a matter of the soul's satisfaction – our souls, and God's. If our soul is *"straight or right"* we will live and walk by faith. If our soul isn't *"straight or right"* God's soul *"has no delight or pleasure in"* our drawing or shrinking back. Our Heavenly Father can never be content with us being contaminated, constricted, and held back by fear and faithlessness. The journey that we, the righteous are called to walk, includes adjusting in adversities and also requires faithfulness and fearlessness. Faithfulness is neither optional, nor a luxury item – faithfulness must be our *lifestyle*!

There is a Chinese Proverb that states, "The journey of thousand miles begins with a single step." We should never be satisfied, or seduced into thinking that just a single step is synonymous with a journey, or even a walk! We must walk, taking steps, even if we can't see the end of our journey or our destination, from where we are. Dr. Martin Luther King, Jr. said, "Take the first step in faith. You don't have to see the whole staircase, just take the first step." However, we can't satisfy ourselves with one step. He said, "just take the first step" – not just take one step, or the *only* step! In other words, we must *walk it out*! I recently read a Facebook post by Dr. Henry Cloud, that read, "Happiness is found not mostly in the finish line of your goal, but in the journey itself."

We can never enjoy the journey that we don't start – neither can God enjoy or be pleased with our journey unless we *start* it. Essential to every journey (if we really want to please God), is that we make an intense effort to imitate Him by walking in love. In other words, if we want to keep His soul content with us, we must continually obey the command to walk in love. Ephesians 5:1-2 reads, *"Therefore become imitators of God [copy Him and follow His example], as well-beloved children [imitate their father]; and <u>walk continually in love</u> [that is, value one another—*

practice empathy and compassion, unselfishly seeking the best for others], just as Christ also loved you and gave Himself up for us, an offering and sacrifice to God [slain for you, so that it became] a sweet fragrance." (AMP) Verse two in the Amplified Classic reads, *"And walk in love, [esteeming and delighting in one another] ..."* The Passion Translation reads, *"And continue to walk surrendered to the extravagant love of Christ..."* (emphasis added) Walking continually surrendered to His extravagant love will ensure that His soul is satisfied.

We've been given multiple invitations and a multitude of incentives to go after and obtain the life God offers and expects us to obtain. Therefore, this is the time to either go get it, or get back up, and then go get it! We can no longer remain blind or forgetful of what was already done for us. Here's a reminder of why we must go get the life that was prepared and promised to us: *"But anyone who fails to go after these additions to faith is blind indeed, or at least very shortsighted and has forgotten that God delivered him from the old life of sin so that now he can live a strong, good life for the Lord."* (1 Peter 1:9 TLB)

It's "All We Can Eat!", Family. Let's Love Virtuously!

Chapter 15
Revisiting The Very Reason

"For as these qualities are yours and are increasing [in you as you grow toward spiritual maturity], they will keep you from being useless and unproductive in regard to the true knowledge and greater understanding of our Lord Jesus Christ."
(2 Peter 1:8 AMP)

It's All We Can Eat!

Before Apostle Peter concluded that there were various qualities contained or prepackaged in us, he prefaced the above Bible verse with these four simple, yet profound words: *"For this very reason..."* (see 2 Peter 1:5) Other translations read, *"This is why..."* (CEB), *"Because you have these blessings..."* (ERV), *"Yes, and for this very cause..."* (WEB). I'm reminded of another simple reason my mom, older sister, other parents in my neighborhood, and even my Teachers and Coaches would say: "Because I *said* so!" Can you relate to that?

I wonder if Apostle Paul was simply relaying the same message to us, but in a more subtle, but loving way. After all, our Heavenly Father *did* "say so", when He spoke us into being. He told the Prophet Jeremiah, *"Before I formed you in the womb I knew [and] approved of you [as My chosen instrument], and before you were born I separated and set you apart, consecrating you; [and] I appointed you as a prophet to the nations."* (Jeremiah 1:5 AMPC) The Voice reads, *"Before I even formed you in your mother's womb, I knew all about you. Before you drew your first breath, I had already chosen you to be My prophet to speak My word to the nations."* The CEV reads, *"Jeremiah, I am your Creator, and before you were born, I chose you to speak for me to the nations."*

Before we were formed in our mother's womb, and prior to us being presented to or premiering on the planet, our Heavenly Father preferred, preordained, and prepackaged us with everything we would need for our prophetic assignments! That's part of the *"very reason"* why He can expect us to execute what He has established and assigned us to do. Like everything else in creation, we are products – the produce or fruit of His spoken Word. In other words, both our origin or our beginning and our being, is because of His *"Let there be..."* and *"Let Us make..."* Even to this day, His powerful Word holds the universe and us together (see Hebrews 1:3 and Colossians 1:17).

The other part of the *"very reason"* is because our Heavenly Father finishes what He begins – He completes what He starts! That's because He sees the says the end of a thing at the *beginning*! Before the words *"In the beginning..."* (see Genesis 1:1) were ever spoken, and eventually written, there was *evidence*! And everything that ever existed and even what will eventually exist, had and end! God had saw it and spoke it!

It is written, *"<u>Declaring the end and the result from the beginning</u>, And from ancient times the things which have not [yet] been done, Saying, 'My purpose will be established, And I will do all that pleases Me and fulfills My purpose,'"* (Isaiah 46:10 AMP) Other translations in part read, *"<u>At the beginning I announce the end, proclaim in advance things not yet done</u>; and I say that my plan will hold, I will do everything I please to do."* (CJB) *"<u>From the beginning I told you what would happen in the end</u>. A long time ago [From ancient times] I told you things that have not yet happened. When I plan something, it happens [...saying, "My counsel will stand"]. What I want to do, I will do."* (EXB) (emphasis added)

I really wanted to move on. However, the Holy Spirit wouldn't release me, until He reminded me of some other verses or promises pertaining to Him seeing and finishing before the beginning: *"I am the Alpha and the Omega, the First and the Last (the Before all and the End of all)."* (Revelation 22:13) Other translations read, *"...the Beginning and the End [the Eternal One]."* (AMP), *"...the*

First and the Last, the Beginning and the Completion." (TPT), *"...I'm A to Z, the First and the Final, Beginning and Conclusion."* (MSG)

The Holy Spirit also reminded me of the Apostle Paul's promise in Philippians 1:6: *"And I am convinced and sure of this very thing, that <u>He Who began</u> a good work in you will continue until the day of Jesus Christ [right up to the time of His return], <u>developing [that good work] and perfecting and bringing it to full completion</u> in you."* The Message reads, *"...the God who started this great work in you would keep at it and <u>bring it to a flourishing finish</u> on the very day Christ Jesus appears."* (emphasis added)

Finally, the finishing touch on the topic was when He reminded me of our instructions to look to The Lord: *"Let us look only to [keep our eyes on] Jesus, the One who began [<u>Pioneer/Founder</u> of; or Leader/Prince of] our faith and who makes it <u>perfect [completes it]</u>."* (EXP) Other translations read, *"...we focus our attention and expectation onto Jesus who <u>birthed</u> faith within us and who leads us forward into faith's perfection."* (TPT), *"...Jesus, Who is the Leader and the <u>Source</u> of our faith [giving the first incentive for our belief] and is also its <u>Finisher</u> [bringing it to maturity and perfection]."* (AMPC), *"...Jesus, who is the <u>Author and Perfecter</u>..."* (AMP), *"...the <u>Initiator and Completer</u>..."* (CJB) (Hebrews 12:2 emphasis added)

That, in itself, should give us all the reason we need to both, run our race and rest in His *finished work*, simultaneously! However, the *"very reason"* is very layered. One of the layers is identified as *diligence*. Diligence directs us into effectiveness and productivity. In fact, diligence is a *prerequisite* of our prosperity! The book of Proverbs provides us with a few perspectives on the progress of the diligent, and perils of those that disregard diligence. Here are a few examples:

> *"The hand of the diligent will rule, But the negligent and lazy will be put to forced labor."* (Proverbs 12:24 AMP)

> *"Poor is he who works with a negligent and idle hand, But the hand of the diligent makes him rich."* (Proverbs 10:4 AMP)

> *"Do you see a man diligent and skillful in his business? He will stand before kings; he will not stand before obscure men."* (Proverbs 22:29) The Passion Translation reads, *"If you are uniquely gifted in your work, you will rise and be promoted. You won't be held back— you'll stand before kings!"*

Diligence does more than cause us to *"stand before kings"* – it will also cause us to *"stand before"* and be in the proper or right *"relationship"* with The King of Kings! One Hebrew word for *"diligent"* is *charats* or *charuwts* (khaw-roots). It's defined as "sharp" or "pointed." It can also mean "decisive, determined" and "eager." Another Hebrew word for *"diligent"* is *mahir* (maw-here). It can mean "quick, prompt, ready, skilled."

In order for us to advance and be effective in our endeavors, it requires energy and effort. It's not enough to just possess the traits or qualities that God gave us. We must *exercise*, *multiply*, and *increase* them. In order to do so, we must be *diligent*. This is why we were informed, *"For if you possess these traits and <u>multiply them</u>, then you will never be ineffective or unproductive in your relationship with our*

Lord Jesus the Anointed;" (2 Peter 1:8 VCE emphasis added)

Other translations or versions that emphasize our obligation to earnestly exert effort and energy, in order to be effective or productive read, *"... <u>multiply them</u>..."* (VCE), *"active and growing"* (MSG), *"... <u>keep growing</u> in this way..."* (CEV), *"for these things <u>existing and abounding</u> in you..."* (DRBY), *"...are <u>increasing [in you as you grow toward spiritual maturity]</u> ..."* (AMP) (emphasis added) This, again, is dependent upon us being *"diligent"* – being *decisive*, *eager* and *determined*.

As I alluded to, earlier; this is a *partnership*. God did His part, by *imparting* to or depositing in us, the gifts, traits, virtues, qualities, etc. In other words, God has deposited virtues in us, in order that we participate, partner, or be partakers in His *divine nature*. Their effectiveness or productivity is dependent upon us doing our part, through our diligence; *abounding, growing, increasing,* and *multiplying* in them! When we are obedient in these areas, we obliterate any opportunity to be *"useless and unproductive"* (AMP), *"inactive or fruitless"* (TPT), *"ineffective or unproductive"* (VCE), *"inert nor unfruitful"* (YLT), or *"complacent or unproductive."* (PNT) Instead, by remaining diligent – being skilled, ready, and sharp, we make our *"lives useful and meaningful"* (CEV) or *"productive and useful"* (NLT). This should not be seen as hard work. Instead, we should look it as *a labor of love*!

It's All We Can Eat!

It's All We Can Eat! Let's Love Diligently!

Chapter 16
What Happens When We Live God's Way

"But what happens when we live God's way? He brings gifts into our lives, much the same way that fruit appears in an orchard—things like affection for others, exuberance about life, serenity. We develop a willingness to stick with things, a sense of compassion in the heart, and a conviction that a basic holiness permeates things and people. We find ourselves involved in loyal commitments, not needing to force our way in life, able to marshal and direct our energies wisely."
(Galatians 5:22-23 MSG)

It's All We Can Eat!

The core Scripture passage for this chapter, and for the book series, for that matter, asks an interesting question. Fortunately for us, like a thoughtful Teacher, the answer to the tough question is immediately answered for us! What I like about this interpretation of Galatians 5:22-23 from *The Message*, is that it takes it from what may appear to be an abstract description of love, and translates it into demonstrations or displays of actions, attitudes, and activities. In other words, it gives us a visual of the virtues of love.

Another version that paints a vivid picture or gives us a visual of the value and virtues of love listed in Galatians 5:22-23, is The Passion Translation. It reads, *"...joy that overflows, peace that subdues, patience that endures, kindness in action, a life full of virtue, faith that prevails, gentleness of heart, and strength of spirit."* These amazing aspects are all the *"fruit of the Spirit"* or the *harvest* of love. They are a complete *crop*, which must be cultivated in us *collectively*. We can't pick and choose which ones we want to consume, and which ones we want to cast aside – which ones we want to receive, and which ones we want to reject – which ones we want to dine on, and which ones we want to decline – which ones we want to reap and retain, and which ones we want to refuse. It is an indivisible diet plan – there's no separations or substitutions!

They Want To Know What Love Is!

So, as you can see, and I'm sure that you've heard before; "Love is a verb – love is an *action* word!" In fact, love is God, and love is also *God in action in us*! I was reminded of a song by the rock band Journey. The title of the song is *I Want To Know What Love Is*. The lyrics in the hook are, "I want to know what love is. I want you to show me. I want to feel what love is. I know you can show me." I believe that there is a world full of people, both Believers and non-believers, who *want to know* and *want to feel* what love is. However, if they're ever going to experience *knowing* and *feeling* love – specifically, the love of God, it's going to be shown and felt by it *flowing* through our *participation* and *demonstration* of love.

We're going to have to stop and invest some time to think things over. Seeking wisdom, understanding, and insight from our Great and Generous Jehovah. With discernment, must read between the lines – hearing even what's not said, and growing wiser as we grow older. There are mountains we all must climb, while carrying weight upon our shoulders. Yet, we must endure the journey through the fog and under the clouds, experiencing the love of God that keeps us warm as life grows colder.

We'll encounter those, whose lives have experienced heartache and pain, and they don't know if they can face it again. We must be there to encourage them that they can't stop now – they've come this far, under stress, through struggles and strife. Reminding them that God has been with them, even when they thought they were living a lonely life. They want to know what love is. They want us to show them. They want to feel what love is. They *know* we can *show* them!

We'll invest the time God has given us to look around, to see and hear those among us. We have nowhere left to hide, and our *assignments*, who are in need of love have finally *found* us. In our lives, there's been heartache and pain. Yet, we count it not loss, because of what we learned and also gained. That's why we can tell them that they can't stop now – they've come this far, through the storms and

210

rain. We can introduce them to Love, Who can ease their every pain. They want to know what and Who love is. They know we can show them. They want to feel what and Who love is. They *know* we can show them!

As we look around, are we readily available to lift the burden from someone else's shoulder? Are we willing to be a covering or provide the warmth, when someone else's life grows colder? We all have races to run and our race courses include mountains we must climb. In spite of the mountains to climb and the races we must run; are we ready *always*, to offer hope and encourage, cheer, and coach others – even if it appears that they are closer to completing their course or climb, than we are?

I thought it was interesting that the last part of the hook in the song says, "I *know* you can show me." Much like the sentiments of the songwriter, I believe there's a world that knows, or at least, have been led to *believe* that we can show them love. Therefore, it is imperative that we present or show them what true love is. We can't be like the fig tree that displayed leaves, and *appeared to* or *gave the impression* that it had produced fruit (see Mark 11:12-25). But upon further inspection by the Lord, our Chief Fruit Inspector, the fig tree was found to only have leaves! As a result, it had to suffer the consequences of being cursed and withering away.

We cannot afford to be like the fig tree. Neither can we afford to be like those the Apostle Paul warned Timothy about in 2 Timothy 3:5 when he wrote, *"holding a form of [outward] godliness (religion), although they have denied its power [for their conduct nullifies their claim of faith]. Avoid such people and keep far away from them."* (emphasis added) When we are content to just have a *"form of godliness"* and denying its *power*, we are also denying others the opportunity of obtaining, knowing, and feeling love. In other words, when we refuse to allow others to be revived or refreshed by the fruit of the Spirit – when we don't display, demonstrate, or distribute what was deposited in us – when we don't do what we're supposed to do *"for one of the least of these"*, we're also not doing it for the Lord! (see Matthew 25:40-45)

Those were a couple of examples of what happens when we do not live and love God's way. They were rather unexpected since I did not have that in my notes. However, that's how the Holy Spirit often shows up in my writing and speaking. It would appear to be unannounced. However, He has an open invitation to instruct me as He sees fit. I've grown to love and expect the *real-time revelations* and *direct downloads* from my Daddy!

That leads me into my next point. Just as important as questioning what happens when we live God's way – when we love and live the life designed for us, using what He deposited in us; is knowing the consequences of disobeying or disregarding the life He designed and the gifts He deposited in us. Although the above examples should suffice, I'm going to dive deeper, below the surface for some other reasons why we should live our lives (which are really not our own) God's way, and the consequences of not being content and conformed to His will and way.

Without Love

In 2 Peter 1:8 we are assured of what we can expect to experience when engage in the life that was established or arranged for us. It reads, *"For as these qualities are yours and are increasing [in you as you grow toward spiritual* maturity], <u>they will keep you from being useless and unproductive</u> in regard to the true knowledge and greater understanding of our Lord Jesus Christ." (AMP) I'm not sure about you, but this is enough to excite and encourage me! We've been prepared, programmed, and prepackaged with an energy that *increases*, as we engage in pursuing, knowing, and understanding Christ *more intimately*! This same embedded, preprogrammed, implanted, power, as it increases, prevents us from becoming unfruitful, useless, and unproductive. In other words, when we obey the prompting or provoking of what's prepackaged in us, it prohibits us – it precludes any propensity for us to impersonate or imitate that *"wicked, and lazy, and idle"* servant in Matthew 25:26!

I'm also excited and encouraged because this also informs me of the facts and truth that I have been equipped and empowered to not only to be *fruitful* and *productive "in regard to the true knowledge and greater understanding"* of our Lord, but it also makes me aware that I have the ability and responsibility to show others "what love is" by demonstrating it in a way that they "feel what love is"!

In some cases, I am able to show them what love is, because they *know* I can show them! I can only know how to show them, because I have continued my pursuit of *knowing* Him! Another version reads, *"...they will keep you from being inactive or fruitless <u>in your pursuit of knowing Jesus Christ more intimately</u>."* (TPT) This not merely the concept of *continued education* – we must be constantly enrolled in *lifelong learning*!

And because we are constantly learning, we are continually reminded to obey or keep the command to *"Always be ready to give an answer when someone asks you about your hope."* (1 Peter 3:15) (CEV). Some other translations read, *"Be ready to speak up and tell anyone who asks <u>why you're living the way you are</u>, and always with the utmost courtesy."* (MSG) *"And if anyone asks <u>about the hope living within you</u>, always be ready to explain your faith."* (TPT) (emphasis added) We can readily respond this way, because we realize that it is The Christ in us, Who is *"...the hope of glory."* (Colossians 1:27)

The last value or virtue listed in 2 Peter 1:8, pertaining to what happens when we live God's way is that we are *"able to marshal and direct our energies wisely."* In other words, we will walk in wisdom. Walking in wisdom warrants sharing our knowledge and wisdom. What we learn, we must also be willing to share with others – we shouldn't withhold what we have. We are commanded, *"Do not withhold good from those to whom it is due [its rightful recipients], When it is in your power to do it."* (Proverbs 3:27 AMP) Other translations read, *"Why would you withhold payment on your debt when you have the ability to pay? Just do it!"* (TPT) *"Never walk away from someone who deserves help; <u>your hand is God's hand for that person</u>."* (MSG emphasis added)

Although these verses were written in the context of owing someone money, I believe it is a principle that can be applied to the knowledge and wisdom that we possess. I also believe that it is our responsibility to share it with those who are in need – *"rightful recipients"*, in the same way we have a responsibility to share or show love to those who are in need. It is a *"debt"* that is due – that we owe to others.

Romans 13:8 reads, *"Owe nothing to anyone except to love and seek the best for one another; for he who [unselfishly] loves his neighbor has fulfilled the [essence of the] law [relating to one's fellowman]."* (AMP) Other translations read, *"Don't owe anything to anyone, except your outstanding debt to continually love one another, for the one who learns to love has fulfilled every requirement of the law."* (TPT) *"Let love be your only debt!..."* *"Owe nothing to anyone—except for your obligation to love one another..."* (CEV, NLT in part, respectively, emphasis added)

Refusing to show love and share wisdom are serious offenses. In fact, our Heavenly Father considers them a sin! James 4:17 reads, *"So if you know of an opportunity to do the right thing today, yet you refrain from doing it, you're guilty of sin."* (TPT) So, rather than close our eyes to the opportunity to do the right thing, we should take advantage of the opportunity to be a blessing, by placing others in an advantageous position.

The Apostle Paul put it this way: *"So then, as occasion and opportunity open up to us, let us do good [morally] to all people [not only being useful or profitable to them, but also doing what is for their spiritual good and advantage]. Be mindful to be a blessing, especially to those of the household of faith [those who belong to God's family with you, the believers]."* (Galatians 6:10 emphasis added) The Passion Translation reads, *"Take advantage of every opportunity to be a blessing to others..."*

When we take advantage of each occasion and every opportunity, we are essentially, planting or sowing seeds of good. And in due season we will reap a harvest. A harvest that is so huge that we won't even be able to handle it all, by ourselves. It will resemble God's response to our tithes and offerings, and also what receive as a result of giving to others. In other words, God will *"open the windows of heaven for you and pour you out a blessing, that there shall not be room enough to receive it."* (Malachi 3:10) When we do good, as well as when we give, it will be given back to us with *"good measure, pressed down, shaking together, and running over..."* (Luke 6:38) This is what happens – how our Heavenly Father and mankind responds when we live God's way.

Without God's Way

When we live God's way, we *"walk in the light"* (1 John 1:7). We not only have our physical eyesight, but we also have *vision*, which allows us to see beyond what can be seen with our natural eyes – we see into or get a view of the future. When we live God's way we also are able to walk in the light because we have His Word in our heart. His Word is a lamp to our feet and a light to our path (Psalm 119:105). Therefore, as we live and as we walk, we are able to let our light *"shine"* – not only for us to see, but also for others see and *"glorify God"* (Matthew 5:16).

However, when we're not committed to walking His way, the consequences are quite the contrary! Instead of having the eyes of our *"heart flooded with light"* (Ephesians 1:18), we will find ourselves suffering like those written about in 2 Peter 1:9: *"blind—shortsighted [closing his spiritual eyes to the truth], having become oblivious to the fact that he was cleansed from his old sins."* (AMP) The person that walks this way – in darkness, is also not walking in truth or with *"The Truth"*! What's worse is that this is a choice to suffer self-imposed inflictions to be sightless and truthless! In other words they make a decision to be *voluntarily visually impaired and imprisoned*!

It's All We Can Eat!

I say that this is a choice or decision because this particular verse reads *"closing his spiritual eyes to the truth."* Other translations read, *"But those who don't grow in these blessings are blind."* (ERV) *"The man whose life fails to exhibit…"* (PNT) *"But those who fail to develop in this way…"* (NLT) *"But if anyone lacks these things, he is blind, <u>constantly closing his eyes</u>…"* (TPT emphasis added) As you can see from these other examples, the person who is ineffectively living God's way is doing so, either *ignorantly*, or *intentionally*. Everything that our Heavenly Father deposited in us or imparted to us, was done so with the intention and expectation that they *increase, expand,* and *be exhibited* in us. He gave or *gifted* them to us, and it is our responsibility to cultivate, grow, and increase in them! In other words, he made the deposits, and it's our duty to diligently. *develop* them!

I want to share with you that I was the person that I've been describing here, for most of my life – including most of my Christian life! I could try to sugarcoat it, saying I was suffering from short-sightedness or near-sightedness, but the truth of the matter, if I may put it bluntly; I was *blatantly* blind! As I was studying for this chapter, I stumbled upon the footnotes in The Passion Translation. Here's what I discovered about blindness – walking in darkness or not *living God's way*: "Although the Greek word *myōpazō* can mean "nearsighted," it is a compound word taken from the base word *mystērion* (mystery), and *optonomai* (to look upon, to behold). The implication is that when the virtues of the divine nature are not flourishing in believers, it is because they are "closing [their] eyes" to the mysteries of our faith."

When the virtues of the divine nature are not flourishing in us, our Heavenly Father is not pleased with us. We were placed on this planet to be partners and participants – *"partakers of the divine nature"* (2 Peter 1:4). It is an intrinsic and irrefutable factor of our faith! If this *nature* is not working, it's because *we're not working it*.

Love Is All We Need!

On the morning that I was writing this section of the chapter, I had a conversation with the Holy Spirit. As I was standing at the sink, making tea around six in the morning – seemingly still half asleep, I heard him say, *"Faith works by love."* (Galatians 5:6) My response was, "Yeah, I know. And without faith it's impossible to please God." (Hebrews 11:6) Holy Spirit repeated His first statement, *"Faith works by love."* I stood there for a few seconds, stirring honey into my tea, thinking about what He had just said to me…*twice!* All of a sudden, the sleepiness slipped away from my mind and body, and I said, "Oh yeah - *now I get it*! So, what You're saying is that faith works by love, and although without faith it's impossible to please God; *without love*, I won't have the faith *needed* to please Him – without love, it's *impossible to have the faith to please God*!" If the Holy Spirit would have had a mic, He would have dropped it right there in my kitchen sink!

So, just to make sure that I got the message, He sent me into the dining room to write down the dialogue or what I would describe as a *download*. I picked up a pad that I rarely use to write on. It was from the Sandals Resort. After writing down our discussion, He led me to read the logo at the bottom of the pad. Just below the logo, are the words "Love Is All You Need". I can't tell you how many times I walked back and forth between my dining room and the kitchen, smiling and shouting, "Love Is All I Need!" Later that day, He prompted me to post on social media, "The Just shall Live and Love by Faith!" Yup, yet another "mic drop moment" from The Holy Spirit!

He is absolutely *all* we need, to do all that He has called and commissioned us to do. One of the things that He has called and commissioned us to do is be *developers*. The first area or construction site that we're called to cultivate or designated to develop is *ourselves*. You may be asking, "What do I need to cultivate or develop myself?" I'm so glad that you asked! The answer is simple: *Love Is All We Need!* However, I have to give you a heads-up: Love may not look like what *you're used to Love looking like*! I learned this the hard way. Nevertheless, I am thankful to God that I learned – that I *finally* got it!

Love looks like and in fact, is *patient* (1 Corinthians 13: 4). Patience is definitely needed to develop ourselves, be developed by God, and also for us to deal with or endure others, who are also being developed. It's a process that isn't always pretty. In fact, at times and during some seasons, it can be pretty painful and often perplexing! Therefore, we must *"let patience have her perfect work..."* (James 1:4) in us and also in others.

We are Developers! We are in a constant process of building, configuring, constructing, edifying, evolving, expanding, etc. It's a fact and truth that we must face and move forward, in the finished work of Christ. We do this – we develop through being fortified and fueled by His Love or patience. This is why it is written of about us, *"We develop a willingness to stick with things..."* (Galatians 5:22 MSG) I'll elaborate on this expression of Love in Volume 5.

It's All We Can Eat!

    Concerning development, I heard something that still resonates with me years later. One night during Bible Study, Elder Andrea Harper (an Intercessor and Teacher in our Ministry) said, "God wants to develop our spirit, so that we can override our flesh." I had to post that on social media immediately, with the caption: #WaitOnWisdom (WOW)! It is so true. We must override and overrule our flesh or *our way*, and the only way to do this is with Love, or *"the fruit of the Spirit"*, and one of the expressions of His love is *patience* – patience to be *developed* and to develop.

    When we patiently and persistently wait on wisdom, we will receive what we need to develop and willingly endure whatever comes our way. In other words, when we let patience have her *perfect work and perfecting way* – when we live God's way, we will receive wisdom and love. *"He brings gifts into our lives, much the same way that fruit appears in an orchard..."* (Galatians 5:22 MSG) We will also be *"perfectly and fully developed [with no defects], lacking in nothing." – "complete and whole" – "become mature and well-developed, not deficient in any way."* (James 1:4 AMPC, TPT, CJB, respectively, emphasis added)

It's "All We Can Eat!", Family. Let's Live And Love God's Way!

About The Author

Robert L. Warring, Sr. is a native of Chester, Pennsylvania. There, he serves as one of the Elders and Bible Study Teachers on staff at Life In Christ Ministries. He has attended there since 1993, under the leadership of Bishop Dickie and Pastor Tina Robbins.

He is a graduate of Chester High School Class of 1979, and Christian Stronghold Baptist Church's Christian Research & Development, where he studied Biblical Counseling.

He is an avid reader, student of the Bible, Author, Mentor, Poet, Speaker, Entrepreneur, and also the father of 4 adult sons: Anur, Robert, Rick, and Mike.

He is also the Founder and CEO of Trini-t-Wear, International, which is a Christian Activewear company that promotes the Gospel Message with the use of t-shirts, hats, and sweatshirts.

He is the Author of "The Kidnapper & The King's Kid: Strategies For Avoiding Spiritual Abduction Volume 1". This is his first in a series of Spiritual Warfare manuals. It is both an autobiographical and instructional tool that teaches strategies to help the reader, as well as assist them in rescuing others from struggles that have held them captive. It is filled with over 275 pages of power-packed principles to Prepare, Empower and Preserve!

He's also written "It's All We Can Eat!: *Feasting On The Fruit of the Spirit*" Volume 1 Fair & Legal. He is currently writing volumes 3 (Joy), 4 (Peace) and 5 (Patience), as well as the paperback copy, "UnAware: *The Untold Story of Adam & Eve*". This is a follow-up to "The Kidnapper & The King's Kid: *Strategies For Avoiding Spiritual Abduction*".

It's All We Can Eat!

Contact Information

www.warringglobalpublishing.com

warringglobalpublishing@yahoo.com

Facebook: Robert L Warring Sr

Twitter: @Wordz2LiveBy1

Instagram: @wordz2liveby1

TikTok: @robertwarring551

Snapchat: wordzwarrior

www.ingramcontent.com/pod-product-compliance
Lightning Source LLC
LaVergne TN
LVHW020927090426
835512LV00020B/3239